VENDOR MANAGEMENT

An insider's strategies to win and create long lasting change

By Agostino Carrideo

First published in 2015 by BTM Group Pty Ltd
Level 27, 101 Collins Street, Melbourne, Australia

©BTM Group Pty Ltd
The moral rights of the author have been asserted.

National Library of Australia Cataloguing-in-Publication data:

Author:
> Carrideo, Agostino

Title:
> Vendor Management – An insider's strategies to win and create long lasting change

ISBN 13:
> 978-1514315200

ISBN 10:
> 1514315203

Subjects:
> Vendor Management
> Leadership
> Culture

Editor-in-chief: Maria Martello
Cover Design: BTM Group

Disclaimer: The material in this publication is of the nature of general comment only, and does not represent professional advice. It is not intended to provide specific guidance for particular circumstances and it should not be relied on as the basis for any decision to take action or not take action on any matter which it covers. Readers should obtain professional advice where appropriate, before making any such decision. To the maximum extent permitted by law, the author and publisher disclaim all responsibility and liability to any person, arising directly or indirectly from any person taking or not taking action based on the information in this publication.

Dedicated to my wife, Geena, my daughters, Siena Lily and Giulia Sage and my parents for all their love, support and inspiration.

To all my professional colleagues who I have shared joy and pain with in delivering vendor management, I invite you to read and adopt the learning's in this book and join me in the movement that culture enables strategic vendor management.

Table of Contents

Foreword

Are you a person who likes to make it happen?
Are you a CEO, CFO, CIO or Business Owner?
Do you value control and certainty over your business and its growth path?
Do you consider yourself an innovative leader utilising best practice technology?

This book is for all the business visionaries out there who believe that there is always a better way to innovate and improve their business. Whether you are growing your own business or working within an organisation. This book is for you.

I want you to join me to disrupt everything that is wrong with the current old school disempowering business culture that is running rampant and adopt the new wave of empowering strategic collaboration. No more "What's in it for me?" but "What's in it for we?". Company culture has been the missing link in enabling effective vendor management and that is why poor mismanagement exists today. For decades companies have been spinning their wheels not achieving the business results that they have set out for. Wasting money, time and precious resources in doing so. You are not alone, in my 20 years as a vendor management practitioner I've seen the effective vendor management and poor vendor mismanagement that exists today.

I believe in focusing on culture, people and the strategic systems to support them. By doing this companies are able to effectively leverage their existing resources, streamline information and communication allowing them to boost their profits and mitigate business risks with their third party vendors. Evolving to strengthen strategic alliances between businesses. In order to achieve this, it is crucial that all levels are in alignment with their corporate values and beliefs creating a sustainable and even more profitable synergies between strategic partners.

PART 1

CHAPTER 1

Leadership Affects Culture And Culture Affects Vendor Management

What Is Great Leadership?

> "Control is not leadership; management is not leadership; leadership is leadership. If you seek to lead, invest at least 50% of your time in leading yourself — your own purpose, ethics, principles, motivation, conduct. Invest at least 20% leading those with authority over you and 15% leading your peers."

> *— Dee Hock*
> *Founder and CEO Emeritus, Visa*

I know that you are wondering "how is culture linked to vendor management practices? and it's a good thing to wonder because that means you are reigniting your quest for learning best practices and all the things I am about to share will be easy and cost effective and that will simplify your vendor management program. Imagine that I am engaged with your organisation sitting right next to you telling you all this now, all the activities that you can act on to finally get certainty which means you have what it takes to manage vendors and lead strategic relations. Now that you can learn this, I am thrilled to provide you with new insights, and new understandings. And you can do this, can you not?

I was so looking forward to writing about vendor management best practice, the emerging revision aptly named vendor risk management and how leadership and culture intrinsically plays its role in ensuring vendor management success, because the organisation is crying out for certainty and significance. The possibility of expanding a business function role to act as vendor manager ambassador, removing the costly resource bottleneck, and enhancing vendor engagement. I'll introduce the new era of web based business intelligence tools for effective and efficient vendor management.

So what's my pitch? Disrupt old school thinking because it's not all about systems and processes for vendor management. Which means as you implement the best tools, people and processes, the higher-level culture with all its levels of thinking ultimately influences the experience all parties receive. When parties come together, and mutually invest in culture alignment, it opens the door to strategic relations and closes the door on all the poor excuses of the past. We do not need to do it the old way because we have always done it like this. I'm sure you'll agree, if you're a selfish and erratic driver on the road, buying a new BMW sports car will not make you drive with grace and ease!

Leadership, Culture, Values and Beliefs. All of these core attributes have significantly affected my ability to drive best vendor management outcomes in my engagements. Organisational culture directly impacts the success of vendor management whether or not you gain access to innovation. More than likely your nearest competitor which has aligned their own culture with their clients will gain the commercial advantage.

In the past 20+ years, I have gained deep vendor and contract management experience in the following industry sectors: Information Technology and Telecommunications (IT&T), Business Process Outsourcing (BPO), Procurement, Energy, Banking, Mining, Defence, Management

Consulting, Aviation. I have been exposed to a wonderful array of leadership styles and cultures and it's this variety that has equipped me to share some further thoughts on leadership.

"There's a difference between knowing the path and walking the path" Morpheus, The Matrix

Reflecting on my broad vendor management experience it is the organisation's culture that fosters win-win collaborative relationships between the organisation and their third party vendors. This has been the key difference between saving millions of dollars and minimising exposure to business risks. One of my most rewarding career highlights was my role with KPMG Australia (2002-2004) as the National Manager for IT Vendor Relations. I had many late night calls engaged with my European counterparts working on exchanging best practice vendor relations strategies and working on global sourcing initiatives. My peer's authentic personal culture was a direct match to me, it must have been my Italian heritage and the amount coffee I was drinking at the time to stay awake for the calls. We just spent hours discussing how to leverage strategic relationships and the access I received to vendor executives and the implementation of shared initiatives, forged and cemented my reputation as the "What's in it for We and not Me" amongst the vendor community. Their model at the time was to have a definitive line in the sand for strategic sourcing and relationship management, each with their own strategies and supported with a shared information management system. I had just graduated with a Masters in Information Management and Systems, so the fact that

I could apply my learning immediately just stretched me even further.

It took another decade for me to experience the same passionate desire to affect relationship management. All other engagements said they wanted to apply best practices, yet with no mandate to affect the underlying cultural issues, they seemed to just fizzle out. They were just another transactional engagement. So in 2014, I was engaged by Australian Pure Play Procurement Management Consultancy. The engagement was to develop for Telstra a best in class Supplier Relationship Management strategy and framework for the procurement group. The culture was being highlighted for change, this change had CEO sponsorship, and was a strategic initiative by the CEO. The minimum requirement was set. It's a start. The privilege to contribute to best practice was rewarding. I certainly look forward to serving more clients in building truly collaborative relationships.

Ok, I can feel tension in my body as I start to think about the not-so-great cultures I have had to experience. So instead of dragging up poor examples I would prefer to share the attributes defined later in this book under the Psychology of High Performing Teams. In this model, it details how a great culture can in just 2 weeks move from 'Start' to a 'Lost State'. I am sure you have experienced some if not all of these 'Lost State' attributes;

• Low interest in the mission

• Expectation of lack of consistency by the leader

- Leader drives everything

- Deadlines missed

- Results not the focus, busyness seems to matter

- Focus on tasks, and 'jobs' and what has to be done

- Excuses, blame, lack of accountability

CHAPTER 2

We Need To First Understand The Attributes That Define Values, Attitudes, Beliefs And Emotional Aptitude

So how do we bring life to organisational culture? How do we effectively align with 'like' cultures? Or how do we inspire cultural alignment with our strategic partners?

We need to first understand the attributes that define Values, Attitudes, Beliefs and Emotional Aptitude. These all influence our ability to experience our own culture and the culture of third party vendors.

So how do we change the Culture? How do we maintain a context where innovations and creativity are encouraged? How do we ensure that we have an organisation where the high performers are invited and welcomed, and know they are in the right place? Good people won't appreciate this as much. Great people will. Attitude is, in terms of culture, the approach people have to what is being done, what needs to be done, what isn't being done and what could be done.

It's the question: 'How does that person or third party vendor approach a new task?' With enthusiasm? With doubt? With resistance? With gossip? With care? With caution? With a get-on-with-it attitude? These littlest indicators tell us so much about people.

When something needs to be done, and it's not that pleasant a task, who does it and what's their attitude towards it? I pay very close attention to my strategic partners' behaviours in these circumstances. This is where you learn exactly the experience you are receiving, from personal values from the vendor account manager, or is it a true reflection of their own organisational culture? This reveals so much.

What about when there is enormous pressure coming in from an outside source such as a third party that your employees can't control and influence? How do they respond? Do they complain? Do they hope it will pass? Do they hope they won't have to do anything? Do they ask if they can help, but not really mean it? Do they find out how they can help and then do it? Do they find out how they can help, do it, and get others to help also?

The attitude we have during the good times is predictable, but not a predictor of attitudes during the tough times.

As a leader, I must know I can rely on the people around me through all kinds of weather, including the storms. This includes the many third parties we have partnered with. You know ones who declared that they're in the relationship 100% and that this time it's going to be different because they have full executive support at the contract signing dinner? Yes I rolled my eyes too or did you break out with a laugh?

When it's sunny, everyone is out on the deck.

When the winds come up, some people complain, some head downstairs to wait it out, and some people set the sails and get busy.

And when the storm hits, who is left on deck are the people who are going to save lives. You'll even be surprised by who they are, and when it comes to the external third parties, are any parachuting onto the deck from their sunny beach to save you? Well they better be as that's the belief and culture I aspire to empower in all of my vendor management engagements. Strategic partners should be more like marriage, for better or worse. Yes you can have your arguments but you work out how to move forward, put it behind you and do your best to not fail again. Ok you didn't like the marriage analogy, let's look to sport then. The season is played out in full at their best capacity no matter what the results are. If you're not on deck in the storm, then, you can get off my deck when the storm clears and the sun comes back out.

Attitude is the quality of approach to anything that needs doing. The attitude you're looking for in your organisation and in your strategic vendors needs to be or include the following:

- Proactive

- Initiative

- Enthusiasm

- Willingness

- Can-do

- Tenacious

- Disciplined

- Never need reminding

- Tells it like it is

- Sees it as it is, not worse or better than it is

- Holds up the standards when you're not there

- Expects others to hold up the standards

- Uncompromising

CHAPTER 3

What Is High Performance Culture?

The role that organisational culture plays in the development of leaders is crucial and often overlooked. One reason for this is that people at work in general are so embedded in their own cultures that those cultures become invisible to their conscious mind. Quoting Aristotle, "We are what we repeatedly do". Culture is viewed as the values and practices shared by members of a group.

Organisational culture therefore is the shared values, beliefs, practices and stories – all of which in combination makes a company unique. In order to comprehend further how we can bring culture to the surface and the benefits of organisational culture in developing future leaders, we ask the question "Why is culture important?"

Why is culture important?

Today, modern organisations view culture as synonymous with building a company's brand. There is good reason behind this forward thinking notion as well. A survey conducted by Deloitte (2012) showed that 94% of executive and 88% of employees believe in the importance of having a distinct workplace culture in business success. The survey also found a correlation between employees in a well-defined and unique-cultured organisation with those who feel "happy at work" and "valued by company". When a leader shares the brand's nomenclature, they stand as the driving force behind creating, building and guiding the success of the company.

WHY?

UNITY: Culture provides a sense of identity. The more clearly an organisation's shared perceptions and values are defined, the more strongly people can associate with their organisation's mission and feel like a part of it.

DIRECTION: Culture provides people with a sense of direction. Employees set their personal benchmarks and expectations based on a joint belief and shared interpretation of what his or her responsibilities are. More importantly, culture influences the direction of employees' developmental goals. We not only set personal benchmarks at work, but we hold team members accountable in raising the team's benchmarks. This serves as a positive driving factor for employees to continuously engage in self-development.

STANDARDS: Bigger than any employee's individual interest, culture reminds people of what their organisation is all about. Not only does culture remind employees what their individual standards and expectations are, but culture encapsulates the responsibilities beyond that of individual roles. The culture we find ourselves in affects policies and procedures throughout the organisation and the decision we make as a company.

GROWTH: Organisational culture is possibly the best indicator for an organisation's capacity, efficacy, and longevity. It also contributes significantly to the organisation's brand image (to the world) and brand promise (customer service). For example, having core values that embraces change and innovations paints a picture of an organisation that is willing to progress and adopt new methods where change is demanded. This shared attitude amongst employees will propel the company to a new level of success. We take for granted how culture can improve our performance as leaders and motivate us as a team. While the visible aspects of culture are often easy to spot, it usually takes much more time and effort to understand and appreciate the importance of the invisible.

However, it is usually the invisible elements of culture that have the most impact on the way people view the organisation and as a result, how they view an organisation's marketing strategies and whether or not they accept or reject your product or service. The effective leader appreciates the value of culture as a powerful influence over people's behaviour and therefore the results that they deliver.

CHAPTER 4

Beliefs Are What We Think
Is True

Beliefs are what we think is true, about ourselves, our colleagues, our team, our organisation, the market, people and life in general. Some people believe they'd rather have everyone like them, than have results. They're not going to be a great leader. Some people believe that results must come and that to do this everyone is needed and valued. Some people believe working after a certain time is 'overtime' and won't do it unless paid for every minute. Some people believe that a great day is completing what's started and won't leave until it's done. Some people believe that the only way to succeed is to step on other people.

Some people believe that the only way to succeed is with and through other great people. Some people believe that a great day is one of collaboration and talking, rather than delivering. Some people believe that a great day is delivering, rather than talking and collaborating. I'm confident that one or more of these beliefs matches your own map.

There are 1,000's of beliefs for any situation. And all of them will shape and determine how successful your culture, and your organisation can become.

I have seen many organisations introduce systems which simply were not needed. The system was going to address the issues identified by the consultant. Yeah right. That worked. So the revolving door kept revolving. Sound familiar?

On the more effective example, I have seen organisations actively encourage morning and afternoon tea breaks, stand and stretch times at 3pm on a daily occurrence, surprise employees with ad hoc fun activities, award great contributors, lunch breaks are a must, going home early, taking time off if you did extra work at the end of the day, and letting people know they were overworked and their commitment was noted and appreciated.

You may already see where this is going.

We do the hours we want to do. We're built like that. No one makes us stay back after mere mortals leave.

And what we do in hours is nothing compared to the truly phenomenal teams – there were days when the Apple designers went all night and did seven days a week... for weeks, to get the design perfect.

I just let out a huge sigh. My career affords me the opportunity to work across many industry verticals and I have seen a rapid change and the above Apple example is under threat. After a while, committed employees to the business become disillusioned. So commitment and productivity diminish. The culture awareness is not addressed, and the typical result is more people got hired to fill the drops in results. New people filled seats, and produced nothing. Every project deadline and productivity benchmark was being missed! The organisational soul had left. So what happened? A new belief structure was taking hold amongst the tribe.

THEIR BELIEFS:

- Work is 9-5 and that's it

- Past 9-5 don't expect too much of me

- You can't expect too much of me

- This is just a job

- If I'm not told about something, don't expect me to figure it out

- If I've only been doing something a short time, you can't expect anything of me

- I don't like pressure

- I will decide what pressure is and push back

- No one can be the boss of me unless I like it

- It's more about being liked/good looking/egotistical than about results

- No one knows my troubles and if you did you wouldn't ask anything of me

- Feedback is criticism and you're a bully

- You're a bully if you ask me to do something I don't know how to do, even if you show me how to do it

- No-one understands me and everyone asks too much of me

The last belief is the ultimate externalisation of the problem. You hire monkeys, expect the place to go bananas.

I do not tolerate this for too long, I encourage these people to move on, this is the time for organisations to focus on installing their true beliefs that lead to a great culture, great results, high-performing teams and everyone feeling awesome about what they do.

Beliefs that are living, lead to results. And they're way more fun to have than the (negative) beliefs I've listed.

I know that there are companies out there filled to the brim with people who harbour the beliefs I've just listed. I just know it's not the type of beliefs that attract the best people, so how on earth can you expect the best delivery, and attract the best clients, have the best business, and drive the best results?

BELIEFS THAT TEND TO GET GREAT RESULTS, BUILD A GREAT CULTURE AND ATTRACT AND INSPIRE THE BEST PEOPLE:

- There's always a way

- There's always a better way

- If it's going to happen, it's up to me

- I am responsible for this and I love it

- You can count on me

- When the going gets tough, I turn up ready to get it sorted

- When the going gets tough, I have to set the example of excellence for everyone else

- No one makes me have a bad day, I do that all on my own

- I am here to be the best I can be

- I love success

Whatever your beliefs (and you can have any belief you want, obviously) you are shaping the culture around you. If you constantly share how hard everything is, you're going to have an impact.

If you constantly share how you're making progress, that too will have an impact.

We are always projecting our beliefs onto the world around us. As leaders, it's up to us to ensure we project the very best beliefs that enable those around us to become the best version of themselves they can become.

CHAPTER 5

The Culture Changer - Emotional Aptitude

How can personal emotional aptitude be related to business? What does this have to do with vendor management? How do you turn off emotional aptitude when you first enter your office building in the morning?

I am always intrigued by human behaviour and how we internally represent events that occur in our lives. The fact is we all have emotions. Actually we all have lots of emotions. Some of us feel it's our 'right' to express them, and you can, wherever and to whomever you choose. Others believe that there is a time and a place for expressing how we feel.

Some just never express emotion and take on the poker face approach to life, yet expect us to know how they're feeling at any given time. An apology if that's you. Top marks for being self aware, many people simply aren't! And there is every shade of emotion and expression of emotion in between this.

The person who (1) manages their emotions, (2) expresses appropriate emotions, (3) remains calm under pressure, is generally the person to rely on when it comes to stressful moments.

If people are not encouraged to respond this way, when the pressure is on, they will respond anyway they want to, which means having to spend time managing people's emotions, rather than the crisis.

EMOTIONS WHICH NURTURE A GREAT CULTURE:

- Focus

- Calm

- Calm pleasure

- Enthusiasm for others

- Enthusiasm for a project

- Enthusiasm for progress

- Consistency of moods

EMOTIONS WHICH DETRACT FROM A GREAT CULTURE:

- Cynical expressions of disbelief

- Defeat

- Lack of energy

- Apathy

- Stand off-ish in moments of triumph

- Disapproving looks when people are spontaneous

- Grouchy or moody

- Inconsistent moods

- Blow ups or flare ups of anger

- Judgmental attitude and feelings of ill-will

- Hostility directed at someone or something

- Sulking

I'm sure these lists are not surprising to you. What I have witnessed is how many people don't give feedback to team members when they behave in a way that is hostile or inappropriate to a functional team. Why not? That comes back to the culture and its response to Emotional Aptitude.

Language Preferences

Every day we interact and build relationships with everyone we meet. Have you ever considered why it is that you just 'click' with some people and others you just don't and why we, ourselves, think and act in a certain way? It all comes down to our own internal representational system: which means how we represent the world using our senses.

We have the following senses to rely on when processing information:
What we see = Visual modality
What we hear = Auditory modality
What we smell = Olfactory
What we sense/feel =Kinaesthetic modality
What we taste = Gustatory
What we tell ourselves = Auditory Digital

We use our visual, auditory and kinaesthetic modalities most often when making sense of our world. For example; we will feel what is good (K), we will see what you mean

(V) or we will hear a bell ringing (A) when something clicks. Some people are primarily auditory digital, which means that they want to know how something works (AD).

We use a combination of these modalities when communicating with others and ourselves.

There are primary modalities (senses) that influence how we learn and how we experience the world around us. Understanding these modalities enables us to understand how we process information and also to understand how others are interpreting the world around them and what they are experiencing. Modalities are also sometimes called representational systems.

THE THREE CORE SENSORY PREFERENCES ('MODALITIES') ARE:
Visual (V) = Sight
Auditory (A) = Sound
Kinaesthetic (K) = Touch

Modalities are important for building rapport and understanding the true identity of others. BTM Group Strategic Collaboration programs includes the essential role that modalities play in creating a high performance leadership teams and third party strategic relationships.

CHAPTER 6

The Four Levels Of Leadership

There are Four Levels of Leadership that ultimately influence an organisation's ability to build strategic relationships both with internal business units and strategic partners. I subscribe to the theory that leadership is not learned through study, yes a first class Master of Business Administration (MBA) is designed to raise the bar on leadership, but authentic leadership is learned like life experience by effectively doing it. How many times have we heard the term "It's like herding cats". Real world gained experience galvanises leaders to deal in these corporate political circumstances especially found during business restructures and large transformational programs. Leading vendors and internal business stakeholders is a delicate process and requires vision and tenacity.

There are no shortcuts on learning how to lead, and there are many pitfalls and mistakes to be made, regardless of your intention and ambition to be a successful and effective strategic collaborator. The difference is great leaders are prepared to make mistakes and many more mistakes than they would like. The result? They have gained a higher level of wisdom along the way. And they are certainly not super human, they were just as scared as the rest of us. They just crossed their fear boundary and moved forward. They accepted and walked with the fear.

Because leadership success is detected through the success of a team, it's relatively easy for a self-aware person, to gauge their leadership abilities. The following section describes the four levels of leadership characteristics.

Level 1: Reactive Leadership is where the new, inexperienced leader hopes people will do what they should, doesn't see they are the cause of the confusion in the team and is constantly frustrated by the lack of results.

The leader 'hopes' the team does the 'right thing'.

Level 2: Dictator Leadership is where once the leader gives up on 'hope' ever being an effective strategy, the leader generally moves into the 'dictator' phase of leadership. It's at this stage the leader becomes distant from the team, distrusts them, thinks they're incompetent, unless they do well and perform, in which case, the leader takes all the credit.

So why does the leader have such low trust? The leader has low trust because they have failed in the Level one phase. To get the team to be effective, the leader draws on the belief that if they do the job themselves then the job will at least get completed.

The team who are more than likely a united tribe have lower performance, tension and momentum. The only hope at this level is that there is a back up manager mentoring the team and keeping them on track.

Level 3: Action Leadership is where you have a team you need to guide for day to day results and development of the team, and strategic thinking is not part of your agenda.

Action leadership holds a strong belief that they need to be able to do the task well and have a high expectation that others need to do it. They haven't yet developed the ability to inspire action in others without demonstrating competence themselves.

At this stage of leadership development hierarchy, the prerequisite is to master 'Action' leadership before progressing to 'Optimal' leadership.

Level 4: Optimal Leadership is leadership where the leader needs minimal guidance on a day-to-day level. They may have a CEO who provides guidance for strategic direction, but most of the time is spent getting on with the job they excel at, and reporting and managing 'up' to the CEO and board so they know they're tracking on agreed targets.

Simply, Optimal leadership is the ultimate goal for all leaders who are ambitious to demonstrate their growth, contribution and abilities.

CHAPTER 7

Levels Of Thinking

Level 1 (by-product of the poor culture)

Have you ever experienced or know someone who has arrived at work looking over their shoulder thinking today is going to be their last day. The negative result of this thinking is the disruption to others and the lack of accountability for their roles tasks and duties. The person who feels this way typically comes from a low trust, no certainty and closed line of communication.

Level 2 (by-product of the poor culture)

The first time the team feels part of the community, driven by leaders and only making decisions when there is full consensus of the community, when it is very safe with no risk taking. It is how it is and always will be. The result of this environment is no creativity or innovation. They are very much told what to do, never stepping out with suggestions for improvements.

Level 3 (by-product of the poor culture)

The person who loves the community but has a burning desire to give something else and they leave the tribe and move on with selfish power. It's all about them and this is where a lot of the corporate games are played. The outcome is very disruptive as the team members are not their focus. There is a what's in it for me only, get out of my way mentality and it's needed to create energy and movement and can be functional level 3 players. Not a sustainable energy.

Level 4 (by-product of the neutral culture)

All about systems and structure. It's about following a system and procedures. It's the red tape and the got to go through right channels mentality. The outcome is very black and white, very wrong and right, it's very this is the way it is and will remain this way.

Level 5 (by-product of the positive culture)

All about results. Very ecological. What's good for me, and what's good for everyone else? How do we all-win? Very outcome driven and have a good time doing it. The outcomes are for the first time about people in flow, and on the mission and looking out for each other.

Level 6 (by-product of the positive culture)

It's about everybody else. Their purpose is to serve everybody else and in fact it has always been about everybody else. They are not fixed to any position and are simply there to bring most value, and if somebody has the capabilities to do it, they will step aside and move to where they are most needed next.

CHAPTER 8

Build Trust For High Performing Teams

I have to say that one of the most valued assets of any organisation is the level of trust they have obtained from the tribe. It's effectively organisational currency, and more valuable than any real currency going at the moment, even gold. If you're not convinced of that, try being in a business where your employees have zero trust. Your business will be extinct in no time at all.

With low trust, and high suspicion, employees, both internal or third parties, tend to hesitate, only do what they have to and put off or avoid decision making altogether. People avoid accountability, or resent it when it's there.

It's worse. I have witnessed a number of people who prefer manipulation and gamesmanship, attracted to and thrive in a low trust culture. They love the politics. They quickly get the 'upper hand' and that's how they like it. It stops being about getting things done, and becomes more about who did what to whom.

In a high trust culture, things happen with grace and ease. People don't have to double guess themselves. They don't waste time chasing information because the organisational transparency means all the information they need to make decisions is available and readily shared.

"Don't just frame your Vision, Mission and Values on the wall. Share and live them by Example", Agostino Carrideo, Founder and CEO, BTM Group

I wish to share my own company values. I am very clear and dedicated to these values. I am focused on ensuring that my company culture thrives on these *values* with purpose, grace and ease. My 3 core Values are as follows:

High Ethical Standards

A business of high principle generates greater drive and effectiveness because people know that they can do the *right* thing decisively and with confidence.

Better Decisions

When facts are overlooked, ignored, or undervalued, they have a way of inexorably reasserting themselves. By keeping minds open and alert, a factual atmosphere stimulates better thinking and thus causes a cumulative build-up in better decision-making.

Higher Morale

A business of high principle attracts high-calibre people more easily, thereby gaining a basic competitive and profit edge. A high-calibre person favours the business of principle and avoids the employer whose practices are questionable.

CHAPTER 9

Trust And Accountability

People welcome accountability and feedback because they seek to improve and value the input from others that can help them and this means that where there are results, there can be trust.

I believe if someone is congruent on delivering the mission, and is meaning what they say, and they follow through on commitments, they deserve and will automatically gain trust. The flow on has the tendency to inspire it from others.

Someone who is congruent will do the right thing. There's less fuss around them. There's quiet determination and an air of consistent productivity and delivery on promises. If you recognise someone you know who displays these attributes then I urge you to dig deep and follow their example. How can you not?

CHAPTER 10

The Psychology Of High Performing Teams

It is imperative to inspire high performing teams. When I am engaged as a collaboration strategist, my definition of teams extends and includes all the people I have identified in the relationship engagement map. This activity typically is done for strategic vendors; vendors that have been segmented as high-risk rating or top 10 spend. This map is continuously updated, it is not static, and the map records all relationship engagement touch points across both organisation and strategic vendor. Current contract management practices only ever focus on key people; these may be detailed in the contract schedules as key persons on an account. The relationship engagement map goes beyond this and seeks to capture all daily engagement. I have had experiences where the touch point count has been alarmingly high with the vendor declaring in executive governance meetings that the cost to serve being reported as commercially unviable. At this stage, the vendor manager would immediately commence a contract review audit as per standard vendor management governance practice to determine the delivery gaps versus contracted obligations.

In my business, the application of the Critical Alignment Model[1] is used for our clients where there is leadership sponsorship to empower culture and their high performance teams. An example would be where an organisation may be about to embark on a significant transformation program. A high performing team has one ingredient, no matter what. And this is momentum. A feeling of energy, focus, and determination, all channelled towards a specific and agreed outcome. There's a feeling of anticipation, optimism, and possibility. People support and champion each other. There is high trust, because

---

[1] Sharon Pearson.

results are on the board. There's an expectation that things will not only maintain, but improve. Injection of new possibilities, innovations and ideas occur consistently, and are welcomed. People want to improve, and to find ways to help the business succeed. There is little talk of 'what's in it for me?' and a lot of focus on what works. People deliver results.

There is focus on the process, to get things done. But the process is respected only if it produces the results. Process for the sake of process is not encouraged, expected or rewarded. Busy-ness is not the point. Outcomes are what its all about.

The Stages Towards High Functioning and Focused Teams[2]
(This can take 6 months to achieve)

Start	Next	Getting Going	Established
Low interest in the mission	Early adopters follow conversations on the mission	The majority follow the conversations on mission	Passionate support for what we do and why we do it
Expectation of lack of consistency by the leader	First fast followers take the concept of mission on board	Early adopters initiate the conversations and there is consistent support for it	The whole team contributes with enthusiasm
Leader drives everything	Sporadic support	Mission based conversations increase	The place is a forum of ideas and innovations
Deadlines missed	Deadlines talked about	Deadlines now the focus and individuals are held accountable to them	The focus is on the mission and how to achieve it
Results not the focus - focus does not seem to matter	Results talked about –busy-ness defended	The people who remain, feel sneakily proud that they want to succeed	Deadlines are achieved

---

[2] Sharon Pearson.

Start	Next	Getting Going	Established
Focus on tasks, and job's and what has to be done	People who don't like accountability complain, or quit	Less excuses, more questions, more curiosity about how to succeed	Results are achieved
Excuses, blame, lack of accountability	Excuses, blame and finger pointing (can get worse before it gets better, people don't like change)		A sense of team pride
			Excuses are called out, curiosity, brainstorming, leden lead to actions, not more talk

The Stages of a Low Functioning and Unfocused Teams (this can take 2 weeks to achieve)

Start	Next	Winding down	Lost
Passionate support for what we do and why we do it	The leader doesn't lead the discussion on mission	The majority retract and focus only on tasks	Low interest in the mission
The whole team contributes with enthusiasm	Leader doesn't generate ideas and only responds and reacts to others	Trust wanes	Expectation of lack of consistency by the leader
The place is a forum of ideas and innovations	Leader allows excuses	Certainty drops and confusion rises	Leader drives everything
The focus is on the mission and how to achieve it	Followers pause and hesitate	Decisions get questioned and not actioned	Deadlines missed
Deadlines are achieved	A feeling of uncertainty comes into decision making	Momentum begins to disappear	Results not the focus, busy-ness seems to matter
Results are achieved	Momentum slows		Focus on tasks, and 'jobs' and what has to be done
A sense of team pride			Excuses, blame, lack of accountability

Start	Next	Winding down	Lost
Excuses are called out, curiosity, brainstorming – that lead to actions, not more talk			

[3]

---

[3] Sharon Pearson.

CHAPTER 11

How's The New World
Going To Look?

Just imagine, and it's a good thing to wonder, your high performance culture is supporting best practice vendor management, and drawing on a new set of vendor management ambassadors. Sourcing and contract management activities are now being monitored and managed. That means your work life is a whole lot less stressful. Risk is nowhere near as frightening and a matter of fact. It's just business and you know how to manage and treat these. Reporting information is straightforward. The vendor collaboration and related governance outcomes are now consistent and all performance and communication reporting is accessible across the organisation. Last and not least, you now have a proactive relationship with your auditors and not fearing the repercussions of fines and losing your license to conduct business! Great committed people owning lifecycle management, and the empowering web based tool is in place. You now can finally be a leading example to your industry. Your third party vendors are raving fans. Left the best point to last, all regulatory and compliance is met with ease of reporting for the board.

This is where the game is played. Where courage and thought leadership can truly tangibly bring bottom line differentiation.

What will you learn in this section?

You will learn that buck stops with you. Your culture and employees are more than likely mirroring your values and beliefs. Your strategic vendors are either mirroring and matching your culture or struggling to align their culture with yours. Oh, was that too direct? And I haven't even shared my examples. As an executive peer, I do appreciate the complexity of corporate life. Early in my career, I used to focus on my ego telling me that despite the MBA qualifications and with leadership teams best intentions, no single person can affect the culture. It takes years to change the attitude, beliefs and aptitude. There are many stories of the fierce leaders spending thousands on development management programs, bringing in great skills to inspire the team. Workshops being held mapping out the next year's strategy with wonderful statements aligning to the corporate values.

Why on earth was the strategy cycle not making the quantum changes in feeding great culture we read about? Then I asked myself the question, how many people love and live in congruence with their corporate values and beliefs. It then hit me, the tribe is disconnected from the manufactured text book values. Sir Richard Branson is congruent in his philosophy that it's all about his people. Every week he is a shining example of living his values and beliefs, his tribe believe him and contribute to their value and belief system. I know we've all read his books, but let me offer you some wisdom, the change is within you. And you can make the change. Just let me know when you're ready as I am not on a mission in this book to rescue you.

You want the New World now don't you? There is a model that creates long lasting change.

This model is the Critical Alignment Model.

The Critical Alignment Model is the basis of all BTM Group Strategic Collaboration programs.

Its pretty straightforward, if you and your organisation and your strategic third party relationships cannot learn effectively, you cannot access new discoveries and innovations effectively.

All learning's start with an effective learning strategy. We facilitate the learning strategy, your task, adopt and install the effective strategies across all parts of your lives, business relationships and careers.

The Model's key benefits include;

- Getting everyone involved on the same page and talking the same language

- Giving all participants one common united focus

- Knowing where they are in the observation of a client, vendor representative or a team member

- Knowing where they need to focus

- Knowing where the gaps are

- Knowing best practice to close the gaps

- A model for feedback and growth

The 4 dimensions to the Critical Alignment model.

Environment

The outcome the organisation wants to achieve, the purpose of the outcome, the thinking, the mindset, the standard and attitude needed to achieve the culture outcome.

Structure

What is needed to achieve the outcome in terms of systems, repetitive behaviours, categories of focus, and what are the benchmarks for success.

Implementation

The actions needed to achieve the outcome, how this compares to the ideal benchmark which would be established, to constantly track, check and adjust the trajectory.

People

Who needs to be involved, how they need to be involved, how they are developing themselves to achieve the desired outcome.

PART 2

Have you Said Any of The Following?

► "I missed yet another contract expiration"

► "We need more automated reminders in place"

► "I have no idea who our vendors are or what they're providing"

► "My current process is too manual & time-consuming"

► "Excel can no longer handle our needs"….

► "We need documentation on all our vendors and contracts"

► "Our vendors need to have up-to-date licenses & insurance policies"

► "We have hundreds of vendors — this will take forever"

► "We'd love to off-load some of the work to the vendors themselves"….

► "We need to assign responsibility throughout the organisation"

► "We lack a systematic way of assessing vendor risk"

► "We need to focus on our high-risk critical vendors"

► "We don't have a formal vendor review process"

► "We need executive summaries to share with management & auditors"….

CHAPTER 12

The Excel Approach Is No Longer Good Enough!

Are any of the previous statements currently present in your business? Do you have the following approach in your business?

- An Excel spreadsheet that lists basic vendor and contract information

- A shared network drive that houses all electronic files relevant to the vendors

- The vendor management coordinator manually checks when contracts are expiring and determines next steps

Can the above work? Is it working for you now and will it work for you in the future? Sure, on a small scale. But eventually you'll encounter one or more of the following problems...

- Too much information to reliably and efficiently track in an Excel spreadsheet

- The lack of searching and reporting makes it difficult to get the right information when you need it

- The shared drive becomes completely unwieldy with too many documents and too little structure

- Over-reliance on manual oversight leads to human error that could impact important business decisions

- You spend more time fixing the system and creating workarounds than on managing your vendors

Imagine having the vendor management capability that solves all the above problems by:

1. Having a centralised easy to use system capable of handling the necessary review, documentation and supervisory tasks

2. Routine activities conducting vendor risk assessments to determine critical vendors

3. Performing appropriate due diligence given the vendor's risk rating

4. Documenting contract issues and vendor performance

5. Active monitoring and supervision of vendors throughout the relationship

All of this ultimately gives you peace of mind by mitigating third party risk and empowering strategic relationships with vendors.

The complexity of third party relationships, the daily engagements and complex contracts continues to increase. While third parties deliver the majority (60% or more) of revenue, they also account for the majority of company spend. Company leaders continue to worry about the time and cost even though third parties:

• Offer potential cost savings

• Accelerate time to market

• Allow your business to scale more efficiently

• Enhance your product differentiation

• Give you access to new markets

CHAPTER 13

Yes You Can Simplify Vendor Management. Stop Flying Blind!

My passionate message and impetus to write my story is to allow me to share with you how to simplify vendor management. General vendor management has been hindered with little tool advancement, and Excel spreadsheets being the default vendor management database. As a Masters graduate of Information Management and Systems I am always seeking a solution to empower business intelligence, the challenge, using the KISS model, Keep it Simple Stupid! You will find me referring throughout the book to alternate vendor management titles, being vendor management and vendor risk management. These are effectively like models with vendor management being a more established vendor management lifecycle and vendor risk management following the same lifecycle process but with an additional vendor risk rating process.

Let me start by diving deep into a few examples to bring some definition into the life of a vendor manager working within a formal vendor management function.

A typical day-to-day vendor management event
A meeting held at 1pm with your vendor. The one where you delivered a hard message to perform, fix an issue or resolve an invoice challenge in front of the business sponsor. Vendor managers and procurement staff typically have stricter gift policies to comply with when engaging vendors, and as such the vendor manager's engagement style tends to be more black and white and typically influences a transactional level of relationship management. On the other hand, business stakeholders in some organisations are allowed a different level of discretion and as such enjoy the great perks. So on the upswing of vendor relations,

everything is working as contracted, life's good for the business sponsor. When the relationship is not going so well due to say late delivery of outcomes, the vendor manager is handed the baton to deliver the bad cop demand. This type of event is not recorded, and may not even be tabled in minutes and certainly not raised at executive governance meetings. Maybe it is discussed in an email thread. People will remember the event and tend not to remember the value add a vendor may be providing. Why? Because there is no way to centralise the business intelligence of daily vendor communication using Excel spreadsheets.

Totally disconnected!

I have experienced many different representations on how well the vendor is performing. Without any documented minutes. Yeah right, Seriously!

Let me cut to the chase, leave it to the experts. Well, more on that later. There are a select number of people including myself who are formally trained in vendor management, contract management and supplier relationship management. This skill set is usually found in technology, procurement or contract management business units or external consultancies.

Even with this statement, on a few occasions I have been engaged by a business stakeholder to address a commercial issue or negotiate an agreement on their behalf. Typically contract management roles are quite laborious, even with agreement precedents, timings for turnaround for my internal clients is always challenging in closing out agreed terms in a timely manner as there are many variables. Here lies an opportunity to build a number of vendor management ambassadors within the business who have passed a skills assessment. On talking to business stakeholders in the past, they have declared that they held a contract managers role in the past or had skills near equivalent to a general vendor or contract manager.

Time to disrupt the norm with thought leadership. Imagine, being able to double your resource capability? Within weeks? Would you like a pragmatic staff augmentation strategy? Look inside your organisation, with appropriate delegation rights, in certain cases, a business sponsor could finalise an incumbent vendor agreement amendment or negotiation. Of course, for probity compliance, final sign-off would always be handed back and new sourcing activities would continue to lie under full responsibility of the vendor management or procurement function.

On the other hand, mature sales people have years of experience (and training) in relationship building and continue to invest in ways to close the deal and manage accounts.

There have been numerous times where I have rolled my eyes in embarrassment in a meeting when a business person without years of negotiating experience has given away critical budget information, thinking they are helping the vendor in responding to their immediate needs.

What they fail to realise is, that approach despite all good intentions can directly effect a commercial proposal. A vendor may add further margin to mitigate a higher risk profile being perceived and/or the low balling of a budget number can have the vendor strip out value add and innovation in the hope they win the deal. In some cases the misalignment can have disastrous results where a committed incumbent vendor loses to a new vendor who has received a different requirements brief from a dedicated vendor or procurement manager. In the long term, I have known of like examples costing companies millions of dollars.

If you have access to experienced vendor or procurement resources and the solution you are assessing may be for a major project, consider whether you have delegated authority to sign the deal and ensure your vendor and/or vendor panel are fully briefed on the process of signoff. Engage the vendor manager from day one! That includes preliminary chats over coffee with you account manager. As a minimum, which can work, I have in the past briefed senior business stakeholders on how to proceed and how much to share prior to attending a business led vendor meeting.

So to all the wanna-be deal makers, stop talking please! Yes I have said that on numerous occasions and shut down conversations where commercial advantage and leverage was quickly being eroded and I am referring to early sourcing conversations during a Request for Information (RFI) meeting with a vendor. It is imperative to understand your limitations in the sourcing process. Ask yourself, how many times have I bought this solution in my career, once or twice? Experienced vendor managers are engaged in sourcing goods and/or services on a daily occurrence and understand the commercial and legal boilerplate clause terms that your organisation will sign off.

I also strongly believe that within the business lies an untapped resource pool which may well be qualified to engage as a vendor manager ambassador and as such a strategy to coach and support this pool can empower the business to drive strategic relations without eroding the business end of the third party relationship during a sourcing or issue management event.

After many years working in technology, procurement and management consultancies, all working on the same mission, my remit has been to strip out cost, performance manage vendors and implement best practice governance. It's been a great learning experience. When engaged on the vendor side, the theme of just keep them guessing and never let on that we are working on an elaborate plan to expand the account footprint. Divide and conquer the business, wine and dine the business sponsors. Account managers in droves turn up to the client governance meetings and just buy time in issue management. Normally in both scenarios, the gap between relationship reality and messaging is significant. Organisational executives early in new commercial relationships invest in aligning joint objectives with vendor executives. Then over time their own respective company cultures take over and dictate the level of true engagement. Sound familiar? Ok I hear you say 'that's business'. Yes, yes I get it too. I have had the privilege to be engaged on strategic sourcing programs seeking to implement best practice supplier relationship management. Only the select few organisations are championing this cultural shift. It's a significant investment and change management is pivotal. I applaud these companies.

But what about the small to medium business market? It will be years before the learning from the top filters down? Or maybe not. Maybe they will lead with their nimble size and empower their culture to build strategic collaborative relationships and in the process simplify their vendor engagement and management

This is how I roll. I see myself as the disrupter and thought leader for this market. I am no longer accepting the position statement –it's always been like this!

Let me take you deeper into my experience, I have been engaged by numerous prestigious tier 1 multi nationals, management consultancies and iconic Australian companies in delivering and implementing best practices in vendor management, contract management and supplier relationship management. I have written and published articles in this knowledge domain and sponsored an inaugural strategic vendor management conference. After many years, I just had enough of watching organisations failing to address 2 core-debilitating issues. I must make this statement now, I really respect the organisations seeking to raise the bar on whatever their flavour is, whether it's vendor management, procurement or supplier relationship management. I am confident their vendor community would be behind the maturity uplift and contributing to ensure mutual benefit.

CHAPTER 14

Vendor Risk Management Or Vendor Management?

Ok so let me offer a quick lesson in basic risk management in relation to vendor management. The following will outline this emerging practice of vendor risk management. The ever-increasing reliance on third party organisations is redefining the core driver for implementing a vendor management program. Furthermore, I strongly believe the primary gain is the inherent risk transparency with incumbent vendors on their engagement and delivery. This intrinsically influences the success of third party relationships.

Vendor risk management can be divided into three distinct categories: business risk, control risk, and relationship risk. Business risk deals with the financial, compliance, and geopolitical aspects of a third party's operations.

Control risk addresses the procedures and policies a vendor implements to effectively and compliantly do the job it was hired to do.

Relationship risk differs in that it involves both the vendor and the contracting company. The name itself offers a definition: Relationship risk is concerned with a third party's risk profile in relation to the company that has hired the vendor. This includes scope of services, contract protections, geographic location of services, and delivery—things that the third party does that directly affects the first party.

Relationship risk is also called 'inherent risk': the risk that is inherent simply by engaging in business with a third party. Any relationship with a vendor is inherently risky—a supplier, for example, may not deliver its goods per the contract terms, thus leaving your company without the (potentially important) product. Assessing relationship risk is essential in managing your vendors, especially the ones that are key to your company's successful operation.

Relationship risk management is so important, because it determines:

- What is most important to your company

- How much vendor risk your company will tolerate

- How much risk management will be required

- How much of your resources should be directed toward that management

- When a vendor is simply just not worth contracting

Relationship risk management starts with your company, which must determine which vendors and which functions of those vendors are most important to your organisation. Obviously, a third party that supplies a key component of your product or handles sensitive customer data will be more crucial than the vendor that sells you office equipment. Armed with this knowledge, you'll know what questions to ask during the assessment process.

'Best in class' vendor risk management solutions will allow you to tailor assessments to your specific needs (e.g. providing added weight to categories deemed more important by your company). After analysing the results, your organisation can proceed with managing the relationship risk and, hopefully, improving the relationship between your company and your vendors.

Phew, you might need to re-read that last paragraph. Even with all the fantastic technology available, Excel is still the default vendor management database used widely to manage relationship risk and its just doesn't cut it anymore. Period!

In my business, I espouse the following philosophy, I have a deep belief that Information Management and Communication provides the cornerstone of an efficient vendor management and compliance program.

Why have we focused on this? Technology has finally brought us the era where web based solutions can bring true agility to business on many levels. Agility that is now attainable to many sizes of business. I am excited in the possibilities to finally serve businesses, which would not normally have access to my skill-set and capability. So whilst on a family holiday in 2014 in Thailand, my best thinking happened. I asked myself, what is the recurring issue in each of my engagements? What is it that impedes most organisations? How can we really, at the daily engagement level, bring the 'What's in for We not only for Me?'. What do we need to do to lift the game of vendor relations and automate the management? Every organisation, all sizes, segments and demographics have vendors that believe they can contribute to the 'Why'. In fact, vendors have invested in building engagement models for years to better serve their customer relationships? With this in mind, I told myself, stop sitting on the fence. Become the disrupter. Here I am.

My vision was born and the mission is in place.

1. Empower, coach and support organisations in central-ising and managing their vendors with a risk lens prior-ity in addition to spend.

2. Information management and communication is the silver bullet! Automate using best in class web based vendor management solutions which will power the mandatory processes for effective vendor management.

3. Arm all organisational departments and their identified people who engage with vendors with the information they need to make decisions

4. Share this information with each vendor, that's right; give them the access to collaborate and to mutually own the information, and to be crystal clear for both parties in their obligations to mutually maintain the information.

5. Once the information management and communica-tion is lifecycle managed then second level of maturity can commence. Use the Critical Alignment model to build strategic collaborative leadership and cultures.

CHAPTER 15

Benefits For Proactive Vendor Risk Management

The business case for vendor risk management can be summed up in three words: Do It NOW. That's because vendor risk management is really not a 'nice to have' anymore, it's a mandatory business requirement for doing business. The ever increasing third parties being engaged in delivering day to day operations is now adding a wider risk base. The unfortunate fact to date is many companies focus on vendor risk management as something to be done as cheaply as possible. This is like sourcing recruiting as cheaply as possible, or accounting as cheaply as possible. This negative business approach to vendor risk management can be very detrimental to relationships with vendors and customers and can impact the ability for a company to meet its contractual obligations and regulatory responsibilities where applicable.

In Vendor Risk Management there are other factors aside from cost that businesses can optimise and be proactive about. Instead of using that tired basic Excel spreadsheet and emailing numerous internal and external stakeholders to collect and/or validate information, I urge you to embed culturally all core disciplines of vendor management that will affect your business positively amongst your third parties and its impact will add ease and grace to the daily engagement with your third party vendors. Take a lesson from your internal Sales and Marketing function, mirror the value of information management application in your customer relationship management system.

Here are three benefits of adopting a proactive vendor risk management process:

1. Stay Ahead Of The Regulatory Curve

Companies can use Vendor Risk Management as an opportunity to stay ahead of changes in industry regulations. In most industries, regulations become more and more stringent with each new update, they don't get easier. For example, with the latest PCI DSS 3.0, companies are already scrambling to update their systems and controls to comply with the more stringent security measures relating to credit card payment information security. Companies who proactively manage their vendor risk can stay ahead of regulatory updates as more stringent rules become applicable. Companies that take a reactive approach will be pressed to spend extra time and money on hasty solutions, and may miss strategic opportunities as a result and certainly incur greater compliance costs.

2. Align Contract Terms To Meet Your Compliance and Risk Obligations

Traditionally, contracts with a third party vendor that involve sensitive or confidential data or information will include the following two contract terms: 1) Vendor shall keep all of the information secure, and 2) Customer has the right to review the vendor's security. Businesses should leverage risk up front to build contracts that specify certain controls to outline compliance responsibilities and related service deliverables. Contract terms can indicate when reviews will take place and even set up contingency reviews under certain conditions. For example, a contract might specify that if there is a breach in the vendor's system, the customer will be notified within

30 days. Building appropriate and specific contracts would enforce more rigorous monitoring and controls to meet all regulatory requirements. Without doubt there is no better way to communicate the importance of regulatory compliance than through the up-front contracting process. This offers a vendor the opportunity to adjust their operations and systems to comply, or even, implement a proactive Vendor Risk Management solution to address the management and adherence.

3.   Drive Strategic Vendor Relationships

Taking a proactive Vendor Risk Management approach means you'll be working with the vendor to mitigate risks. A proactive approach builds on setting up specific contract terms by providing reporting, tracking the vendor commitments to mitigate controls and documenting the results. A proactive stance will save the vendor time and money in the long run, making you a more valued client. It is also likely that the vendor has many other clients with security needs similar to yours. The vendor can then build security into its product value proposition, by passing on the process efficiencies and financial savings achieved through your agreement, to other customers. We've seen many examples where a vendor – after a breach and resultant operational changes to improve security – has redone the marketing materials to highlight their commitment to security. These benefits build a compelling business-case to leave the reactive, bare-minimum approach to vendor risk management behind. Companies, who opt for a proactive approach to vendor risk management, will effectively mitigate risks and gain a more efficient and rewarding client-vendor relationship. The real business case for proactive vendor risk management should be: do it NOW, and you can.

CHAPTER 16

Top Ten Must Do Ways To Simplify Your Vendor Management

1. Stop getting beaten up by Auditors

Your auditors want to see that your company has a system in place that does more than store your vendor names and phone numbers.

Imagine being able to accurately review, critical documentation and supervisory tasks that are essential to auditors. A web based vendor management solution can do all this and more.

2. Quickly answer the big-picture questions

"How many active vendors do you have?", "How many of those are high-risk?", "What's coming due?" and "Who owns what?". They can be easily answered because you've implemented a web based vendor management solution, which stores your information in one organised and searchable system with concise reporting

3. Sick of missing yet another contract expiration

Imagine receiving email reminders for expiring contracts at customisable intervals prior to the expiration date. In just one click, you could have access to any vendor contract details from anywhere on any device to your organisation.

4. Streamline and simplify your process

If all your commercial information is scattered across different platforms, departments and email, you're wasting time, money and resources. Get out of the dark ages and consolidate all your data in one place. A streamlined and cost effective solution to your messy out-dated Excel spread sheet. Increasing the productivity of your organisation.

After all, time management is just as important as vendor management.

5. Your homegrown solutions are impacting your decision making

Most internal vendor management systems are a cobbled together mix of Excel spreadsheets, Word documents and shared network drive. This unwieldy setup will only scale your organisation so far. Having access to all the important information is crucial to being able to effectively make decisions. Spend more time managing your vendors than the system itself.

6. Do you know which vendors are putting your company at risk?

The purpose of vendor risk management is to determine your critical vendors — the vendors most important to fulfilling your company's core business functions. Make better use of your time by focusing your attention on the high-risk vendors that can jeopardise your company's reputation.

7. Be prepared for your next negotiation

Make sure you have the information you need to inform your decision-making processes. Grade each vendor's actual performance vs. expected performance, optimise your expenditure. Thorough documentation could be a key advantage during your next negotiation.

8. Know your vendors from the start

Avoid surprises by conducting thorough due diligence upfront such as privacy policies, insurance certificates, references and financial statements. Your high-risk vendors require a more comprehensive review or it could be costing you contract leakage.

9. Unlock Your Business and Share Crucial Business Intelligence

Vendor interactions can take place at many levels throughout your company. Your accounting, IT, legal and compliance departments should all have access to up-to-date vendor information. Have complete control by assigning permissions and limit access to specific modules based on user roles.

10. Access it all from anywhere

As vendor management becomes even more important, you will need greater access to your information. Best in class web-based software enables your centralised information to be accessed on any desktop, laptop, smartphone or tablet.

PART 3

CHAPTER 17

Vendor Management Models

Creating and driving vendor relations and organisational alignment is now more than ever critical on all levels of third party management, where daily decision-making activities are spread across businesses and functions such as technology, procurement, finance, operations, and others. Establishing upfront the governance structures and processes to address misalignments will enable a timely resolution of challenges when they arise.

There seems to be a tendency to adopt the following approach to governance in organisations. They are either centralised or decentralised; both approaches, and other attempted hybrid models of these two can be successful.

The **Centralised Model**, which I have been most engaged in during my career, naturally, keeps most major decisions (such as risk 'tiering' and performance management activities) within a single group, typically a Vendor Management Office (VMO) or similar are found in either technology, procurement or finance business units. While this approach yields a clear and accountable owner, it can have the tendency to generate cultural divide and an undercurrent of tension between the business units that 'own' the working relationship with the third party and the centralised function accountable for vendor management.

The **Decentralised Model** gives rights to the business units that own the contractual relationship to also manage the overall vendor management lifecycle. This too has its drawbacks; it can sometimes result in duplication of resources in undertaking similar activities yet the vendor's experience is fractured as they struggle with mature practices from procurement managers and business unit managers. For example, it's not uncommon to find a major third party supplier engaged on daily occurrence in delivery of services by several business units for very similar contracts and relationships. And a decentralised approach can see inconsistent application and misalignment of vendor management standards between, say, procurement and technology. A hybrid approach, carefully tailored to the organisational context, can help mitigate potential challenges of the other two models, but must be monitored closely to ensure lines of vendor management ownership are not compromised.

The key for successful vendor management lies in an effective escalation framework. I am a strong believer in both parties owning an agreed escalation framework. It needs to be an effective process supported by a best practice tool where both the organisation and suppliers can access the escalation issue and mutually work through their own resolution obligations to address and ensure the learning gained effect a change to mitigate the risk arising again. I have far too many real life experiences in my vendor management career when a great relationship has quickly deteriorated into a primary school yard drama. Sound familiar? Why? More than likely, the real risk and damages is now alarmingly quantifiable. The escalation framework has failed and the lack of centralised information management and communication is now impeding the grace and ease required to get on with these tough and stressful events.

Most organisations currently do not have sufficient expertise, tools and resource bandwidth to address the

ever-increasing additional volumes of third party engagement activities and any arising issues. The centralised
model approach is typically limited with resources, these
resources are spending most of their time in contractual
issues management or engaged last minute by business
stakeholders in a mad rush to close out the latest deal. In
both instances, straining relationships on many levels. In
my experience, organisations need to look to assigning new
responsibilities to the broader organisation rather than create new ones to support third party escalations. So a key
strategy is to invest in an appropriate approach to empower
the organisation when engaging with third parties to be
armed with an agreed line in the sand for its risk appetite
and vendor relations culture.

In large organisations, the architecting of the vendor relations governance model and escalation framework can take
up to six months with another twelve months to 'stand it
up' in the organisation after pilot periods and change management have been integrated.

CHAPTER 18

Vendor Management Frameworks

Effective vendor management is the cornerstone of operational health and cost management. I have found that the six core guiding principles below empower organisations to grow and develop in their vendor relations and management.

- **A comprehensive inventory and engagement map of all third parties with whom the organisation has a relationship.** While most organisations struggle to build this comprehensive list, organisation-wide surveys and centralised vendor management solutions will address the past challenges. Excel for inventory management is flawed. The resource costs in adopting this approach exceeds the investment required by implementing a commercially available web based vendor management solution.

- **A comprehensive catalogue of identified risks to which third parties can expose the organisation**. It's common for organisations to not fully understand all the *inherent* risks their third parties bring in their engagements. A master vendor risk register in a centralised solution is a great way to start categorising the risk information. Risk and Due Diligence surveys can build the information to address the issues regulators are actively pursuing.

- **Risk based segmentation of the supplier base**. Not all suppliers carry the same amount of risk. Organisations need to better triage their suppliers to make sure the most effort is devoted to the highest risk vendors.

- **Rules based due diligence testing**. Treating every supplier the same doesn't make sense. Carefully designed risk rules can help organisations focus their due diligence of suppliers.

- **A disciplined governance and escalation framework.** Third party risk management does not have a single functional owner. Establishing one and giving that group the right decision-making powers is essential. Furthermore, I believe the organisation would benefit by building out a vendor engagement map. With all the external and internal touch points identified, build a culture where there are vendor manager ambassadors in key business units with dotted lines into the overall vendor management function. Apply a skills gap assessment and then develop skills matched to the vendor manager role description, such as one typically employed in a dedicated vendor management function either in Technology or Procurement.

- **Integrated technology, workflow process and web based tools.** Adapting current risk IT applications to third party management in the past was too costly and difficult to stand up the business case, the default has been Excel spreadsheets, or a SharePoint homegrown application. Building a new bespoke tool is even harder and resource dependent. A purpose-built off-the-shelf application is the right answer for many, up in under 24 hours, affordable annual subscription fees, purpose built.

Why wouldn't you do this?

Initial steps to gain quick wins

So if you're on the mission to finally address the flaws in current practices, developing and sponsoring the above six best practices together will form a comprehensive approach to third party vendor management. I believe these critical components must be addressed organisation wide - a collaborative vendor management program. Many of these elements can be built in parallel.

Start with an inventory of third parties

Tighter regulatory frameworks are expecting organisations to have a documented understanding of who their third parties are, as well as a detailed understanding of how each third party interacts with the consumer and the activities it performs.

The many vendor Excel databases are incomplete, and some of the most sensitive risks often turn out to reside in some relationships that are not found and tracked in these Excel homegrown databases. Vendor relationships are often managed in ways with the emphasis on commercial outcomes, with only a secondary focus on commercial risk and mutual relations.

You need to catalogue all third party risks

Stop and listen to this next message. This is really important. *Your third parties can expose their customers, and their customers' customers, to a wide range of risks.* Implementing a centralised vendor risk solution and with simple management of a comprehensive list of these risks and breakpoints is I believe mandatory.

The success of ongoing audits and the scorecard reporting will empower the organisation to proactively monitor and mitigate risk. For example, if a third party Call Centre has a risk of agents misrepresenting product information to customers, their customer will monitor this specific risk in an audit (e.g., through call monitoring) and request regular reports on call quality and customer escalation metrics. Naturally, the inventory of customer risks will vary across categories of suppliers, depending on the nature of the interaction with consumers. Higher risk categories such as IT will typically have 20-30 potential risks.

If I consider the financial industry sector, they may have two challenges in developing the risk catalogue: identifying the relevant risk breakpoints for each category of suppliers, and determining the relative weight and importance of each risk. I would suggest that a master register of risks and their risk weights in each category is broadly relevant to almost all organisations, and can be adapted to the particular circumstances of individual organisations. With the help of the master register, this element can be generally built in three months where resources are applied to a project.

Adopt a risk-based segmentation as a priority

When an organisation is armed with a complete inventory of third parties, assessing their risk weights in each category is broadly a simple system of 'High', 'Medium' and 'Low'. These basic vendor risk categories can finally bring a level of maturity to overall strategic vendor management and more importantly, ensure the terms and conditions in agreements best address the risks identified with mutual commercial outcomes.

In my experience, most multi-national organisations have anywhere between 50 and up to 200 plus high-risk relationships at a time. The high number draws on the many potential underpinning contracts to the vendors contracted. An effective segmentation helps allocate risk management working collaboratively with vendors by conducting more frequent risk and due diligence reviews to higher risk relationships, and conducting routine and potentially automated annual reviews of its lower rated risk vendors.

My preferred model is the rules-based approach, this model simply defines some rules or criteria tied to breakpoints to streamline the assignment to a risk category. This approach is about 40 to 60 percent faster than a score-based approach, as it entails only the risk assessment and due diligence activities needed.

Depending on the size of the organisation, the approach can take 1 to 3 months, and refining it and testing it with business leaders another month or two. Typically a core team of risk experts drives the design, the fine-tuning, implementation and initial survey activities.

What Are Vendor Due Diligence Reviews?

A due diligence review provides assurance that a potential vendor is financially stable, ethically sound and has a mature corporate governance. Reviews should be tailored to the risk the vendor may present to your organisation.

The vendor manager managing the overall relationship should perform vendor due diligence reviews. The assigned vendor manager is responsible for having a non-biased view of vendors and manages the vendor relationship. The business unit owner would typically have the final sign-off on the due diligence review and works with the vendor manager to resolve any outstanding issues.

If your company is currently not performing due diligence reviews, you could be exposed to the following risks:

- Depending on the industry you're in, auditors and regulators could impose penalties, revoke licenses to practice or take legal action against your company if the vendor is not compliant to the standards.

- The press can also damage your company's reputation if a vendor's lack of compliance is made public. This could negatively affect investor ratings, rating agency scores, shareholders and more.

When To Perform Due Diligence Reviews
Vendor due diligence reviews are not only critical when bringing on a new vendor but also to routinely monitor and ensure the vendor has been vetted for any changes from the previous reviews. The goal is to validate that the vendor continues to meet the standards needed to provide their service or product without causing any risks to your company, investors or customers.

Initial Due Diligence Review

Procurement best practices typically mandate due diligence reviews be introduced to the vendors during the Request For Proposal (RFP) process. The RFP and due diligence review should also be used to gauge the vendor's ability to be accurate and timely with their responses. At this stage, both procurement and business stakeholders would monitor closely vendor responses and behaviours from their management and sales representatives, as the vendor's performance at this stage will likely have a strong correlation to future performance.

Subsequent Due Diligence Reviews

This is where the game of strategic vendor management matures. If a due diligence review is only performed during the initial vendor on-boarding, you could still be at risk by:

- Changes in the vendor's management team that could change practices not compliant with contracted obligations, vendor representations during the RFP process and with your initial commercial expectations.

- If the vendor files for bankruptcy, the availability (or lack thereof) of the vendor's product/service could impact internal business stakeholders and/or your core external products and/or services servicing your own clients.

- If the vendor has had any legal actions against them but not directly impacting your company, there is a chance of exposure to both commercial and reputational risk.

My recommendation is simply to mandate annual due diligence reviews across all your vendors — I have found that the best time to perform the review is 6 months prior to the renewal notification notice for multi-year agreements. This should give you ample time to identify any changes that could affect the vendor's risk level. The same questions that appear on the initial review form can be used in subsequent review forms.

When to Change the Review Frequency

Diligence reviews could be done as frequently as quarterly or semi-annually in the following situations:

- The vendor has been classified as a high/critical risk

- The vendor is renewed annually and has been scored high in the previous risk review

- The vendor has been in business less than 3 years

- Items discovered in the last review need to be monitored

- External sources identify risks, such as bankruptcy, vendor redundancies, lawsuits, etc.

Base the Review on the Type of Vendor and Service

Company standards, policies and any regulatory compliance obligations should dictate how many due diligence review templates you should have and how in-depth each review should be, and if one should even be done at all.

To determine how many review templates are needed, it is best to categorise your vendors by function and how tightly they integrate with your company's core business processes.

Here are three sample categories you could have:

Support Vendors

Support vendors may have the longest due diligence review, especially if the vendor handles Non-Public Information (NPI) and interacts with your customer directly or indirectly. This type of vendor most directly reflects your company's public image and needs to be vetted thoroughly.

Focus on:

- Handling of NPI

- Compliance with the Consumer Financial Protection Bureau and Australian Prudential Regulation Authority (APRA) and other regulatory agencies

- Financial review

- Legal review

- Corporate structure and stability

- The vendor's annual spend

Technology and Telecommunication Vendors

The extent of technology-related diligence questions is dependent on the type of product. For example, if the vendor only provides desktop software, then you shouldn't need to ask if they are ISO 27001:2013 compliant. However, you will still want to ensure their support model fits your needs.

Focus on:

- Handling of NPI

- Security of systems (ISO 27001:2013 or similar standard)

- Financial review

- Legal review

- Corporate structure and stability

- The vendor's annual spend

Non-Essential Vendors

Vendors that don't provide direct support to the team may be considered non-essential and probably won't need an in-depth review. A few examples would be your catering, office furniture or garden maintenance vendors. At most you would want to know how long they have been in business and if their insurance meets your expectations. To inquire about their IT infrastructure or how they handle NPI is probably excessive and a poor use of your vendor management resources.

Focus on:

- Financial review

- Legal review

- Corporate structure and stability

How Long Should the Review Process Take?

It has been my experience to allow 10-20 business days for the vendor to complete the review form depending on whether their head office is local or international.

Once the review has been received, it should only take a few hours for the vendor manager to review and input the data into their vendor management solution. I would also suggest you request a Dun and Bradstreet (or similar credit reporting agency) report to validate some of the responses. Depending on the vendor spend/risk, you may want the finance department to review the financials before having the business unit provide the final sign-off of the review.

You should be on the lookout for the following 'red flags' that could remove the vendor from consideration:

- Not completing of the review

- The lack of an ISO 27001:2013 audit when customer information is being handled

- Is currently in bankruptcy or has poor financial results

- Previous or current lawsuits not in the vendor's favour

- Poor credit agency ratings

I invite you to visit www.btmgroup.com where you can access for free an example of potential questions.

What Are Vendor Risk Reviews?

A vendor risk review helps you understand the risks that exist when using a vendor's product or service. Performing a risk review is especially critical when the vendor will be handling a core business function, will have access to customer data, or will be interacting with your customers.

Vendor risk reviews are not only critical when bringing on a new vendor but are also needed to ensure that the vendor is maintaining expected quality standards without causing any risks to the company, investors or your customers.

The goals of a risk review are to:

- Identify any risks the vendor will pose

- Evaluate if the vendor is able to eliminate those risks

- Monitor the risks that cannot be eliminated

- Assess the extent that any outstanding risks may bring to the company

- Determine if your company is willing to accept those risks

Risk assessments are typically a series of questions (or a risk matrix grid), and the answers to those questions result in an overall point value, which then identify the vendor's risk level. A common risk level breakdown is: Low, Medium and High.

When To Perform Vendor Risk Reviews
Initial Risk Review

Risk reviews should be introduced to vendors during the Request For Proposal (RFP) process. Depending on your current RFP process, you may be able to embed your risk review assessment into the RFP. The risk review should also be used to gauge the vendor's ability to be accurate and timely with their responses, especially providing documents you request. Everything at this point should be monitored closely, as the vendor's performance at this stage will likely have a strong correlation to future performance.

Red flags to look out for during the risk review that could remove the vendor from consideration:

- Does not provide any processes for safeguarding confidential data

- Does not perform risk assessments internally

- Does not have a formal security policy

- Does not perform security checks across all functionality

- Does not have a disaster recovery/pandemic plan

Ongoing Risk Reviews

I have found that the best time to perform the risk review is 180 days prior to the renewal notification notice. This normally gives ample time to identify any changes to the vendor's risk level and lets your company respond appropriately.

It has been my experience to allow 10 business days when sending the review to the vendor to complete. Once the review is back in-house, it should only take a few hours for the VMO to review and upload the data into a vendor management software system to identify the risk levels. At this point, you can also compare the current review to the vendor's previous reviews and spot any trends.

How Often Should Ongoing Reviews Be Conducted?

Reviews should be performed according to the vendor's current risk level, such as:

- ○ Low risk vendors: Annually/bi-annually

- ○ Medium risk vendors: Semi-annually/annually

- ○ High risk vendors: Quarterly/semi-annually

You may also review the vendor more frequently than normal if any of the following indicators exist:

- The vendor has been in business less than 3 years

- Items discovered in the last review need to be monitored

- Vendor files bankruptcy

- Vendor redundancies

- Lawsuits that include the vendor

- Negative press releases concerning the vendor

- Lowered ratings by agencies (S&P, Moody's)

- Increased vendor incidents or non-resolution of vendor incidents

Who Handles the Review?

The VMO who owns the overall relationship management should be in charge of managing the vendor risk review process. By its nature, the Vendor Manager should provide the most non-biased view of the vendor, which is critical since vendor's risk level classification will dictate how the vendor is managed throughout the relationship.

If the Vendor Manager finds any high-risk items on the assessment, it should engage the business owner and any other key parties. The result of this discussion can either be:

- The decision maker accepts the high risk level and the vendor risk review is considered complete

- The decision maker does not sign off:

  o The VMO creates an incident for each question that is labelled high-risk

  o The VMO discusses the high-risk items with the vendor and formulates an action plan for the vendor to complete

- ○ Once those risks are mitigated the VMO will complete a new risk review to show the changes

- ○ The revised review is then brought back to the business owner for final sign-off

Base the Review on the Type of Vendor

It is best to create risk reviews based on the services the vendor performs; it certainly doesn't make any sense for every vendor to be subjected to the same review set of questions. Always keep in mind the vendor size and the risk the vendor poses to your organisation — demanding excessive reviews could damage a perfectly functional relationship.

Below are five common vendor types that can be used to help shape your risk review efforts:

- Essential Services - the vendor handles customer data and customer interaction

- Customer Facing - the vendor interacts with customer without handling customer data

- Customer Data - the vendor handles customer data without customer interaction

- Back Office - the vendor supports core services but has no customer interaction/data

- Non-Essential - the vendor does not provide core services or core product

What Are Vendor Performance Reviews?

A vendor performance review assesses how the vendor is performing against Key Performance Indicators (KPI)'s and Service Level Agreements (SLA)'s established in the vendor's contract. It should also show non-contractual performance issues, such as incidents that aren't measured by a service level. For example, you can monitor incidents such as the vendor providing wrong information to customers or other poor customer service.

The goals of a vendor performance review are to:

- Monitor compliance of contractually agreed upon KPI's and SLA's

- Identify areas where the vendor is not performing to expectations

- Partner with the vendor to resolve low vendor performance

- Benchmark the vendor's performance against similar vendors

- Assess performance trends and resolve prior to impacting productivity

- Partner with the business owner(s) to ensure they are engaged with and utilising the vendor's services

Each performance review should have a scoring model that quantifies the performance level. A basic scoring model that I found effective is:

- 0 - Not Applicable

- 1 - Does Not Meet Expectations

- 2 - Needs Improvement

- 3 - Meets Expectations

- 4 - Exceeds Expectations

Why Should I Use Performance Reviews If I Have Scorecards?

Scorecards are one piece of a performance review that tracks the adherence of the agreed upon KPI's and SLA's compared to the larger picture of the vendor's overall performance. Scorecards will not capture all incidents or non-metric related issues such as your company's interaction with the vendor, billing issues or the overall quality of the vendor. Depending on the frequency of the reporting and the vendor's services, scorecards should be reviewed weekly or monthly. Performance reviews should be performed quarterly, semi-annually or annually depending on the vendor's services and their risk level.

Performance reviews may capture data from:

- Scorecards

- Incident reports

- Action plans

- Internal business owner(s)

- Customer surveys

- Prior performance reviews

- Performance reviews from similar vendors

Performance reviews are a perfect way to partner with the vendor for a successful relationship, overall organisational governance procedures are adhered to and to hold the vendor accountable for their performance. If you have not been using performance reviews and have older contracts, this is a perfect opportunity to assess the vendor's overall performance, negotiate better contracts with more defined SLA's and associated penalties.

How Often Should Performance Reviews Be Performed?

Initial Performance Review

Best practice would recommend for new services an initial performance review be performed at 90 days after the services are implemented. This will allow enough time to determine how the vendor is performing and tweak specific KPI's, SLA's and/or implement action plans. If the vendor is not performing to desired expectations prior to the 90 days, each occurrence should be documented as an incident and used in the performance review. If the incident creates a risk, it should be addressed immediately with the vendor by creating an action plan with a SMART (specific, measurable, attainable, relevant, time-bound) goal that will be monitored by the Vendor Manager and business stakeholders.

Ongoing Performance Reviews

I have found that the best time to conduct a performance review is 180 days prior to the renewal notification notice, similar to the risk and due diligence reviews. This normally gives ample time to identify performance gaps to review with the business owners prior to renewing the contract.

When gathering data for the review, it is always a great idea to review the prior performance review to look for negative trending. If the behaviour is evident but not worth terminating the vendor, you may negotiate into the renewal penalties for poor performance and reference back to the trended history.

Using vendor management software to alert you on upcoming reviews is beneficial to the management of your vendors.

How Often Should Ongoing Reviews Be Conducted?

Reviews should be performed according to the vendor's type of service and the impact of the service if the KPI's or SLA's are not met. The frequency of the performance reviews should be set initially with the business owner and the vendor. The review frequency should never change if the vendor is not performing; instead incident tracking and action plans should be utilised for any performance issues between reviews.

- **Annual Reviews** — IT, HR, facility, non-customer impacting vendors

- **Semi-Annual Reviews** — Back office, indirect customer impacting vendors

- **Quarterly Reviews** — Customer impacting and high risk vendors

Who Should Be Included In the Review?

The Vendor Management Office (VMO) should conduct the meeting and include each business owner to review the vendor SLA's that are not met. From that meeting the VMO will objectively score the performance review based on feedback from the business owners. For each low score, the business owner(s) and VMO will decide if the vendor should be placed on an action plan, be put on notice or change the metric to be more realistic.

Once the internal review is complete, the VMO should work with the vendor to work through any low scores. The best way to resolve low scores is to have the vendor create an Action Plan. Partner with the vendor to track the vendor's progress to resolution with SMART goals to ensure both parties obtain the desired results.

Base the Review Questions on the Type of Vendor

Vendor performance review forms should be broken down by the type of service the vendor performs. Their review form should merge specific KPI and SLA questions and generic questions such as: how many incidents the vendor had, how well is their training? Etc.

I recommend that you have multiple performance review forms with specific KPI's and SLA's. With a good vendor management software system you should be able to create a review form with generic questions then copy the form to make service-specific review forms.

Below are four common categories that can be used to help shape your performance review efforts:

- Vendor Performance on categorically agreed upon expectations such as:

    o Key Performance Indicators: actually agreed upon expectations such as performance review efforts, and efficiency and effectiveness of the service

    o Service Level Agreement: actually agreed upon expectations such as performance responsibilities for the delivery of a service

- Vendor Incidents – any incident that disrupts the company's operation

- Vendor Billing – accuracy and timeliness of billing

- Vendor Quality – overall vendor experience to include:

    o Vendor responsiveness – responsive-ness to general questions and follow-up

    o Training quality – quality of training material used for both the vendor and the company

    o Knowledge – knowledge of the vendor's core functions to include the vendor rep, customer service, IT and other departments

    o Vendor innovation – knowledge and adaptability of its services

Using vendor management solution will make it easier to create review forms for specific services, as one review form will not work for all vendors.

PART 4

CHAPTER 19

4 Steps To Getting Started With Vendor Management

Getting started with Vendor Management within a company can be quite challenging. With any successful implementation you need a strategic plan that defines the vision and mission of implementing Vendor Management.

STEP #1 — KNOW THE BUSINESS
Before designing the roles and responsibilities of the VM function you must first know the business and how current vendor relationships are managed.

Questions to ask:

- Why did the company decide to implement a VM?

- What are the current challenges with vendor relationships?

- How does each line of business (LOB) handle vendors?

- Who currently negotiates contracts?

- Where are the contracts, reviews and Insurance Certificates stored?

- Who performs vendor risk and performance reviews?

- Who reviews and submits invoices?

- Who sets up vendors in the company's database or servicing systems?

- Who are the business owners for the vendors?

To answer the above questions, I would suggest meeting with each functional area to discuss the questions above. This would also be the perfect time to set expectations on gathering all vendor documents, understanding the services provided by the vendors, and being made aware of any current vendor incidents and active projects in the pipeline.

STEP #2 — DESIGN and PROPOSE THE VM'S ROLES and RESPONSIBILITIES

The VMO function provides a support role and assists each department with vendor selection, negotiations, contract terms, monitoring vendor performance, identifying risk and handling on-site reviews. Once you have your list of issues, vendors, documents and corporate structure, it's time to create a VMO implementation plan.

DESIGN THE PLAN

Each company will vary on what roles they want the VMO function to be responsible for. The company may not have performed a deep dive into all aspects of what a VM can provide. I would suggest gathering your information from Step 1 and putting a presentation together to present to the executive team.

The presentation should contain:

- Timelines for each implementation phase

- Projected staff size or VRM SaaS managed options

- How you will manage the data

This is the perfect way to validate the business needs and to determine if your VM vision meshes with the executive team's expectations.

VMO FUNCTIONS

After you analyse the company's current vendor risk management approach, you need to evaluate and prioritise what functions you can provide that will eliminate risks for the company and create efficiencies for the lines of business.

I call these the 21 core activities of a VM program led by a Senior Vendor Manager:

- Execution of all NDA's

- Manage RFP's

- Perform due diligence

- Negotiate costs

- Create contracts

- Contract negotiations

- Contract approval process

- Gather business requirements

- Negotiate contract terms

- Manage contract renewals

- Termination of vendors

- Maintain vendor documents

- Risk reviews

- Onsite reviews

- Vendor performance reviews

- Vendor incident resolution

- Invoice audits

- Vendor utilisation

- Vendor setup in systems

- Manage vendor scorecards

- Purchasing/purchase orders

Keep in mind the functions you commit to may require additional staff, depending on the company's volume of vendors.

JOB DESCRIPTIONS

Depending on the initial assessment of duties, you can start creating VRM roles and the set of tasks that each person will perform.

Among the roles you may consider are a contract manager, a vendor analyst and a vendor auditor. Their typical responsibilities include:

Contract Manager

- Assist with the RFP process

- Review and negotiate contract terms and pricing

- Obtain proper approvals and signatures on all contracts

- Maintain and update as needed company standard blanket contracts

- Manage select vendors

- Assist with administering vendor action plans as needed

- Conduct vendor business reviews

- Perform other activities as assigned by the Vendor Manager

Vendor Analyst

- Research, collection, tracking and reporting of vendor SLA's

- Maintain information in the vendor management system

- Track escalated issues and reporting of root cause analysis

- Manage the archive and cataloguing processes for all VM documents

- Tracking of agreement renewal dates

- Assist the team in the collection and analysis of vendor information as input to the annual profit plan cycle

- Perform invoice tracking against purchase orders as directed by the Vendor Manager

Vendor Auditor

- Perform daily activities related to managing regulatory compliance and performance of the company's vendors

- Partner with the Compliance Department to review changes in regulation that may apply to the company's vendors

- Maintain an overall vendor scorecard that relates to vendor risk and performance as related to the review analysis

- Conduct vendor performance reviews

- Conduct due diligence reviews during the vendor on-board process

- Conduct vendor risk reviews as directed by company guidelines

- Perform vendor on-site reviews as directed by the Vendor Manager

STEP #3 - SELECT YOUR VMO SOLUTION

You need to determine how you'll manage all of the information and action items you'll be accumulating. Using a spreadsheet can work as a bare minimum solution, but it proves to be an inadequate solution once you have 50+ vendors and/or need features like document storage and email reminders.

You'll want your VM solution to handle:

CENTRALISED INFORMATION STORAGE AND MANAGEMENT

- Vendor performance reviews

- Risk reviews

- Fully executed contracts

- Vendor certifications

- Insurance certificates

- On-site reviews

- Vendor incidents

- Contract redlines

- NDA's

- Email communications

- RFP results

- Notes

- Miscellaneous documents

TRACKING AND NOTIFICATIONS

- Contract expirations

- Vendor performance reviews

- On-site reviews

- Insurance expirations

- Risk reviews

- Vendor certifications

QUICK REFERENCE INFORMATION

- Vendor contact information

- Contract clauses

- Service level agreements (SLA)

- Cost of services

- Termination dates

STEP #4 — IMPLEMENT THE PLAN

Now that you have the plan approved it's time to put every-thing together. Being in a support role it's imperative that whatever you implement must be simplistic for the business as well as efficient for the VM outcome. Whatever solution you chose, ensure that the business has access to it so you can concentrate on your core functions to support the business.

In implementing any plan you should have policies and procedures for the company to follow and an internal VM policy for your organisation.

VM COMPANY POLICY TOPICS

- Vendor onboard process

- Contract signing authority

- Ongoing relationship with vendors

o Contract renewals

o Performance reviews

o Risk reviews

o Price changes

- o Change in terms

- o Vendor scorecards

- o Vendor issues

- o Gift policy

- How and when to terminate a vendor

VM INTERNAL POLICY TOPICS

- When to use an NDA

- Steps on implementing a new vendor

- How to create and score an RFP

- How to upload new vendors into your Procurement Systems, if applicable

- Creating and managing a risk review

- Creating and managing a performance review

- Processes on managing the vendor management software or database

- How to terminate a vendor

- Contract expiration notification process

- How to manage and resolve vendor incidents

Implement your vendor management solution as soon as possible. The last thing you want to have happen is for high volume or risk vendors contract to expire during this transition phase.

Once you have your policies and procedures published, a repository and tracking system and your staff hired, it's time to officially kick off the VMO function and introduce the policies and procedures and show/present the value you will add to support the lines of business by managing vendor relationships and processes.

Depending on the company culture, you may wish to do a roadshow by starting with the department heads to get their buy in so they can trickle it down to their team, conducting continuing education, or email. I would suggest getting in with your training department and see how they have rolled out new departments in the past.

CHAPTER 20

5 Things To Know About 3rd Party Vendor Reviews

With so many headlines about data breaches, many caused by 3rd party vendors, reading news about security compromises is becoming a too frequent event.

Following the trend of breaches taking months to be discovered, some can take almost a year to discover. Even though many compromises are internal, the impact delay is another reason why vendor screening is so important, especially with key third parties. Australian companies can no longer afford to be in the dark about business details that increase risk. Here are five things you should know about vendor screening:

1. 3RD PARTY VENDOR RISK CAN'T BE ELIMINATED

Although vendor screening is a powerful tool for protecting your company's interests, it is not a cure-all for every threat a third party might pose. Risk can't be eliminated, only managed. Vendor risk assessments can help maximise vendor risk management.

2. THE REVIEW PROCESS DOESN'T HAVE TO BE SO TIME-CONSUMING AND LABOR-INTENSIVE

Executives and risk professionals are hesitant to adopt a comprehensive vendor screening program. Indeed, in years past, assessments consumed much time and energy—resources that organisations simply don't have. However, an automated solution can greatly simplify the process. After assessments are completed, risk staff don't have to waste time tabulating the results because the report gives them everything they need for subsequent analysis and vendor risk management decisions.

3. 3RD PARTY VENDOR RISK SCORING CAN BE YOUR BEST ALLY

Many vendor screening solutions employ risk scoring to quantify the level of risk a third party presents. This innovative solution can make life much easier for perpetually busy risk employees. Instead of poring through pages of assessment results among dozens of reports, you can eyeball the risk score to get an instant idea of how much risk a vendor carries. A low score might mean you can move on to the next vendor. A high score could indicate more analysis will be necessary. Risk scoring might also use colour coding with green for low risk, yellow for medium risk, and red for high risk—to allow you even more streamlined analysis; simply look for red scores and answers to see what areas will need more of your attention.

4. ACHIEVE A COMPLETED RISK ASSESSMENT WITHOUT DEPLOYING VENDOR RISK SOFTWARE

If you don't have the budget or the resources for vendor screening software, or if your staff are so overwhelmed at a certain time of the year that you couldn't possibly undertake another assessment, on-demand screenings can fill the gaps. The process is easy. Inform the vendor risk management service of the third party that must be assessed, and receive a completed risk report within a couple weeks.

5. ROUTINE 3RD PARTY VENDOR SCREEN-ING IS WORTH THE TIME, EFFORT, AND EXPENSE

Nearly half of the major data breaches in 2013 were the fault of a third party. Many of those incidents were tremendously costly—in terms of lost sales, damaged reputations, and disaster control—to the contracting companies that were affected. Due diligence in assessing and managing vendor risk can go a long way in helping protect your company's interests. After all, a third party might be at fault when a risk becomes a catastrophe, but your company's bottom line will ultimately be at stake.

CHAPTER 21

How Does A Vendor Management Office Provide Return On Investment (ROI)?

4 Ways a VMO Can Provide ROI

How Vendor Management Can Positively Affect Your Bottom Line.

A company outsources services to a vendor in the hope that the vendor can perform the duties cheaper, better and/or more efficiently than the company could, thus saving the company money in the long-run. While using vendors is often the desirable way to go, you have to manage the relationship and hold the vendor accountable to acceptable standards.

The VMO plays a key part in increasing your return on investment (ROI) with vendor relationships. Properly utilising a VMO will increase company efficiency, reduce vendor spend and risk exposure, and allow the business units to focus on their core business functions.

While there are no magic formulas in this book to determine exact ROI, using a VMO throughout the vendor lifecycle will provide multiple advantages and ROI in four primary areas.

ROI #1 - Audits

Vendor Invoice Submission Controls
Auditors typically recommend that a review process is in place for submitted invoices. The best practice is to have the business owner ensure and approve that the vendor performed the work, then have the VMO team review

the invoices to ensure costs match the contractual terms. Once approved by the VMO, then the check with purchase order.

Real World Example

During an audit of a department's invoicing process, I saw that that department was only sparingly auditing their largest telecommunication vendor's invoices. After performing an in-depth audit of the vendor, I was able to find erroneous and duplicate charges that totalled $45,000.

Accounts Payable (AP) System Calibrated to the VMO Database

Most AP systems should have controls in place to put a cap on specific expenses, along with an approval process for any exceptions. It is imperative to engage the VMO with vendor invoice fees to ensure whenever prices change or whenever there are new service fees these are validated with the contract terms. If these functions are not utilised, you could be at risk of paying more for services than what was negotiated in the contract.

Invoice Audits

Even if your AP system does extract vendor pricing from active contracts within the VMO database, it is still best practice to randomly audit vendor invoices to ensure they match the current contractual pricing. There are times when pricing may not be updated in the AP or the invoice is submitted under a different code/rate.

ROI #2 - On-Boarding a New Vendor

Adding a New Service

A new vendor should only be selected when the need for their service or product is deemed superior to the in-house alternative. Cost justification (ROI), vendor efficiency and risk also have to be identified prior to selecting a vendor.

The VMO should be engaged as soon as the vendor need is determined. The VMO should review the type of service requested to see if there is currently a vendor that performs the same service in a different department. Eliminating vendor duplication provides a lower total cost by increasing the preferred vendor's volume of services and thus better discount opportunities.

Furthermore, using the VMO as a non-biased party eliminates favouritism and subjectiveness when scoring the RFP, performing due diligence, assessing risk and evaluating the business requirements. By selecting the best vendor in an objective fashion, your company should recognise long-term financial benefits.

Real World Example

I had a request come across my desk to add a vendor for a managed print service that could have been performed by an incumbent vendor. After reviewing with the IT department, it was determined that IT department could add the service to the existing contract and leverage a global discount rate card on the overall contract. This saved the company $88,000 annually versus the proposed pricing.

Contract Negotiations

During contract negotiations, the VMO should have all the requirements, terms and SLA's from the business to negotiate the contract. This frees up the business owner's time during the negotiation process and limits their role to the final sign-off. The VMO should be the company's de facto expert in handling all aspects of negotiating contracts — resulting in the best cost, terms and SLA's.

Real World Example

At a previous company, I saved over $4.5 million annually by renegotiating older contracts. We were able to accomplish this by knowing the business, being aware of current market prices and having excellent negotiation skills.

ROI #3 - Managing the Vendor Relationship

The business unit should handle all day-to-day dealings with the vendor. The VMO should manage the relationship at a higher level to ensure compliance with terms and conditions and work with the vendor to resolve any issues.

Ways the VMO should manage the relationship:

Risk Reviews

The VMO should conduct vendor risk reviews to identify and manage threats the vendor may pose to the company. Risk reviews protect company assets, income, employees, customers, reputation and its investors.

Performance Reviews

The best practice is to use a non-biased party to review vendor performance. The VMO can assess the performance of the vendor by objectively discussing it with all departments that interact with the vendor — or, at the very least, the key stakeholders. A performance scorecard quantifies the vendor's service, quality, efficiency, incidents and SLA's in a manner free of any biased opinions. The performance review should also be shared with the vendor to create a partnership that will deliver results.

Service Level Agreements

SLA's should be identified in the contract and contain material repercussions for the vendor if they don't perform. When negotiating SLA's with the vendor, identify the risks to your business and help set what the penalties should be.

SLA's are only as good as the monitoring of the data — the VMO should handle monitoring, especially if the contract contains monetary penalties. If you are not monitoring SLA's you could be throwing money out the window.

Action Plans/Incidents

There will likely be incidents where a vendor is not performing to the SLA's, has and violated a term in the contract or is not compliant with the risk review. The VMO should work with the vendor to resolve any such incidents so that the business owners can focus on their key functions.

Tracking incidents and monitoring vendor action plans is a perfect way for the VMO to evaluate the vendor at a high level.

Real World Example
I was overseeing a vendor site that had below-average customer service scores. By using action plans and holding the vendor accountable via a formal governance framework, we were able to increase customer service scores by 25 points and elevated them into the top 5 labour augmentation providers.

Vendor Utilisation
A VMO can manage vendor utilisation and reduce costs in several ways:

1. Evaluate all vendors across the company and look for duplication of services. Redundant vendors could potentially be eliminated after a champion challenge and the retained vendor's overall costs could be reduced.

2. Review vendor costs monthly or quarterly to show vendor spend and utilisation. If you notice that a vendor's cost has decreased over time, you can evaluate the vendor's necessity and possibly eliminate them.

3. Review all new vendor requests and ensure the service or product cannot be performed internally at a lower cost or more efficiently.

Real World Example
At a previous company, I identified seven vendors performing the same IT reseller services. We decided to keep

three vendors for benchmarking purposes, eliminated the other four vendors. By negotiating better rates and receiving value added services which were previously invoiced with the remaining vendors, I saved $1.1 million annually for the company.

Management of Contracts and Time Sensitive Data
Contract renewals are imperative to eliminating risk. If a contract is expired and the vendor has an incident, this could expose your company to monetary damages and be a hit to your company's reputation.

Both company-led reviews (risk, performance, and audit) and vendor-led reviews (PCI-DSS 3.0, ISO 27001, etc.) have to be managed and documented. Certificates of Insurance must always be current and provide suitable coverage. Failure to have up-to-date, commensurate documentation could also expose your company to unnecessary risk.

ROI #4 - Let the Business Owners Manage Their Business

The more a business owner can focus on their actual job, the more efficient they'll be and the better the company's performance will be. Properly utilising vendor management to maximise company profits is an intense, detail-oriented process, and shouldn't be part of an employee's overall position.

The VMO should always:

- Negotiate contracts

- Track vendor performance

- Perform vendor reviews

- Manage vendor incidents

- Perform vendor audits

The Business Owners should always:

- Increase sales, customer service and revenue

- Increase department efficiency

- Focus of core department objectives

- Develop team

- Track department performance

CHAPTER 22

Why Is Relationship Risk So Significant?

Relationship risk management first starts internally. Has your company undertaken the steps to segment the profile of your vendors on 'risk' as well as 'spend'? Best practice vendor risk management focuses on reporting to executives vendor risk profiles and scoring. Vital information required to score vendor risk is the documented record of all your vendors, contract terms and what functions of those vendors are most important to your company.

Obviously, a third party that supplies a key component of your product or handles sensitive customer data will score a high-risk rating and will be more crucial than the vendor that sells you office supplies. Armed with this vendor intelligence, you'll know which questions specifically to ask of your vendors during the vendor risk assessment process. Feeling like it's all too hard to undertake in the real world?

New to the market are affordable Vendor Risk Management solutions which are cloud hosted and can simplify the Vendor Management process within your organisation. Delivering management assessments with ease, reach and speed to assist your company in reaching its vendor management goals.

Imagine having access to your vendor risk scores via a web based centralised dashboard accessed anywhere, anytime on your notebook, tablet or mobile. Companies who have implemented Web based Vendor Risk Management solutions have the ability to proactively manage their relationship risk and, more importantly, have the time to invest in maturing collaboration with their strategic third party vendors.

Why you need to embed an IT Vendor Management Office function

The conventional approach to managing IT vendors may not be adequate in the delivery of your new, emerging and disruptive business technology. The shift from the capital intensive IT procurement to the '-as-a-service' model is only one of a number of fundamental changes reshaping the IT services delivery model — globally.

At the core of the '-as-a-service' model, is the need for a far tighter ongoing working relationship between you and your IT service provider as you are now operationally dependent on *their* performance. Implicit in this model is the fact that the provider is now accountable for all the security, operational and other elements comprising the service, over which you have little to no influence or visibility. Their problem immediately can become your headache.

To maintain the operational integrity and alignment between the provider's direction and your requirements in the longer term is no trivial exercise. Once the contract has been signed, and services are up and running, maintaining a healthy and active ongoing vendor management regime will mitigate the risk of losing control.

The vendor relationship landscape is being shaped by a number of factors, some of which are:

1. IT may no longer be the primary decision makers. The tacit understanding that *'because it's IT, IT makes the vendor decision'* is now under scrutiny due to a range of factors including a growing trend of Shadow IT groups,

moves to decentralise enterprise IT or the need to deliver a solution in weeks rather than months to avert a short term business crisis.

2. Your exit is more important than the entry. Under what circumstances can you terminate a vendor's contract, without penalty or prejudice? How painless will be the transition to another vendor at a later date? Plan accordingly.

3. Disruption in your vendor's market: Understand what forces are at play in your vendor's environment by regularly monitoring changes in vendor markets.

4. Too big to talk? If needed, how do you negotiate with one of the globally dominant digital landlords such as Google, Amazon or Microsoft? Will engaging an IT consulting firm or vendor partner be of help in this regard?

5. 'Agile' is the new black: Adaptable, responsive organisations win business and can respond to changes in the commercial, regulatory and security environments. If either your or your vendor's business runs like a Soviet era industrial enterprise, where process compliance is more important than survival will this present a problem?

6. Risk appetite is not constant. In this volatile environment, expect your risk profile to change as your business changes. How will or can your vendor respond — if at all, and at what cost to you?

7. Managing vendor jurisdictions. How well your various vendors play together is key to your overall success. Managing demarcation disputes may be a challenge,

especially if there are non-disclosure considerations between competing vendors that need to collaborate in the delivery of *your* services.

8. Your vendor's shareholders are not yours. Your vendor will make technical, commercial, risk and jurisdictional decisions that are in their best interests. That's called commercial reality, however is sometimes overlooked in the enthusiasm for adopting a compelling new technology.

9. What's the purpose of your contract? Encapsulating every possible change scenario that could occur in your business environment in your vendor's contract is problematic. Stitching up a restrictive contract with your vendor could be counter-productive in an agile, volatile environment. By the time you have to work through enforcing the vendor's compliance to their contract with you, the relationship is probably on its way to being adversarial or dysfunctional.

10. Fragmentation of the vendor's supply chain. Your vendor would most likely have their own vendor ecosystem, so recognise that the challenges *you* face in the selection and management of vendors are similar to *their* challenges. This will continue down the vendor daisy chain. Add to the mix the various IT consulting forms and the web of relationships can become complex, and elevate your systemic risk.

Line-of-business Executives who feel entitled to make enterprise IT procurement decisions should be acutely aware of the forces at play in the volatile IT vendor ecosystem. The sugar hit of apparent short-term success may just set the stage for subsequent failure.

Be informed and well advised, and become the vendor manager in full congruence, not when it suits you.

Companies should manage IT vendors vs. having IT vendors manage the organisation to extract profits.

In the absence of a clear set of vendor management processes and roles in the organisation, vendors are often able to set the agenda and canvass the organisation to increase their footprint and secure added revenue. Major IT vendor relationships tend to have multiple facets and touch points — operational, contractual, financial, executive-to-executive, etc. Through multiple touch points, vendor account teams often 'work the relationship', seeking to protect their existing business with the organisation and make inroads into new areas to build further sales. While the organisation can gain value from consolidating business with key vendors and forming strategic, multi-faceted relationships, such relationships should be defined in a structured transparent manner rather than through a free-for-all sales frenzy based on a relationship without a business case.

Functional or procurement employees are not equipped to effectively manage vendors in a complex IT outsourced environment.

This is one area where dedicated specialist IT vendor management skills are mandatory. While the procurement function may bring resources with transactional or sourcing skill sets, and HR, or Finance operations bring resources with functional and people management skills — none are the best fit for day-to-day IT vendor management in complex outsourced environments. In most organisations, the personnel responsible for ongoing vendor management are the same individuals who drove strategic sourcing and those who managed internal functional departments before they were outsourced. In both cases, such individuals often lack both the knowledge and the skills required to manage complex vendor relationships effectively. Procurement personnel are trained in sourcing methodologies, negotiation, and other procurement skills. Operational personnel have a deep functional understanding and can be excellent people managers; however, they often lack the understanding of what is required to operate in a complex IT outsourced environment.

Hang on, are there too many pseudo vendor managers in the organisation?

There is a common view that inefficiency is introduced as too many employees spend time on unnecessary or redundant interactions with vendors. As companies outsource more activities to vendors, they often find that not all the internal work goes away – and an alarming number of employees across the organisation end up spending time and effort managing and interacting with the vendor. Now as mentioned earlier, this is not going away whilst we have uncontrolled vendor management. It doesn't help now that we have the rise of third party dependence. This overhead is exacerbated by the duplication of vendor management effort that typically occurs across different corporate functions, business divisions, multiple vendors and geographies. The implementation of a vendor risk management system and vendor management coaching throughout the organisation can bring some sense to the duplication and harness the resources. The issue is a by product of departments or functions reaching a tipping point that they are now finding themselves no longer doing the role and managing the third parties as managed service providers.

The disruption in vendor management leadership that I wish to call out is that actual duplication in effort, if harnessed correctly, would in fact arm the organisation with a potential vendor management capability uplift. Unfortunately to date, internal roles and responsibilities are not made clear, because many aspects of the vendor relationships are ill-defined, and because vendors make every attempt to spread their relationship footprint, too many employees which have not been inducted into the skills and vendor management processes, become involved in performing vendor management tasks that are often redundant, inefficient, unnecessary, or even competing. So why is this different to traditional vendor manager dedicated role? For example, technology groups predominately source and run technology. The level of vendor management experience is high due to the nature of the fast paced industry changes and the numerous sourcing events that occur and the high number of vendors engaged in delivering products and/or services.

In my experience this has translated into dozens or even hundreds of employees involved with tracking vendor activities, dealing with issues, and interacting with vendor account teams. The common nightmare for a vendor manager is learning of significant contract breach too late during a business led issue escalation meeting.

I passionately believe Information Management and Communication provides the cornerstone of an efficient vendor management and compliance program. With this mind-set, the effect should marshal the organisation to leverage this principle. Every vendor interaction if managed and recorded in a dedicated system can only serve others.

Depending on the size of the organisation, a dedicated VMO function may not be viable to address the ongoing commercial relationship needs . Therefore, implementing a vendor management solution and taking all the employees which engage with the vendor on a maturity uplift, inspiring and expanding their roles by skilling up with disciplines on general procurement, contract and performance management can best address the needs of the organisation. I stated earlier that there is a common trend around vendor management duplication. Should the organisation have a mature VMO, then the opportunity to expand and grow a number of functional relationship owners into vendor manager ambassadors can offer capability without the hard resource costs. By implementing a coach and support model, the VMO can ultimately monitor and manage the main issue of Vendor Risk Management.

A web-based solution can simplify your vendor management program.

Web based vendor risk management solutions can turn what may seem like a daunting task of managing vendors into an efficient, thorough process that allows organisations to focus on management and analysis rather than hours of catch up. As latest regulatory frameworks and standards gain wider acceptance, due diligence and risk reviews must be updated to reflect the changes as well as any future threats that emerge. The greater flexibility of this iteration also means assessments should be tailored to fit the needs of both company and vendor. An automated solution can achieve these goals in a fraction of the time taken by traditional spreadsheet-based assessments, can reduce the possibility of human error, and can provide a streamlined audit trail to more efficiently track the entire process.

About The Author
Agostino Carrideo

AGOSTINO CARRIDEO, IS THE FOUNDER AND CEO OF BTMGROUP AND THOUGHT LEADER IN VENDOR MANAGEMENT AND STRATEGIC COLLABORATION.

AGOSTINO HAS OVER 20+ YEARS EXPERIENCE IN THE AREA OF STRATEGIC VENDOR MANAGEMENT WORKING IN TECHNOLOGY, TELECOMMUNICATION, FINANCIAL, ENERGY, MANAGEMENT CONSULTING, MINING, AND AVIATION INDUSTRIES. HIS PASSION HAS BEEN TO DEVELOP VENDOR MANAGEMENT CAPABILITIES FOR BUSINESSES, IMPLEMENT VARIOUS INITIATIVES ACROSS THE VENDOR MANAGEMENT LIFECYCLE AND FOSTER A COLLABORATIVE CULTURE THAT EXCEEDS RESULTS.

Agostino's broad vendor management skills have been developed via engagements with large multinational organisations dealing with local and international suppliers, in particular US, Asian and European regions.

Agostino has a Master of Information Management and Systems from Monash University and a Graduate Diploma in Business Technology from Monash University. In addition, he has focused his professional development in the areas of Executive Coaching . His BTM Group Strategic Collaboration programs are designed to empower organisations in their third party vendor management.

BTM Group Services

Become empowered to committed excellence, expand your mindset, embrace behaviour change, and win and create long lasting change. You can create significant shifts in the way of thinking and you can, whilst creating your best results.

Our specialty programs include:

- Strategic Collaboration Programs

- Executive & Team Leadership Coaching & Development

- Business / Personal Coaching, Consulting & Strategy

- Vendor Relationship Management Programs

- Vendor Risk Assurance and Compliance Mentoring

- Culture Empowerment Mastermind Series

- Business Culture Summits

- 1:1 & 1 to many Executive Coaching

- Public Speaking & Key Note Presenter

Join BTM Group movement. I invite you to contact me directly on email.

E: agostino.carrideo@btmgroup.com
W: www.btmgroup.com

Special Thanks

I wish to personally thank the following people for their contributions to my inspiration, knowledge and support in creating this book:

Simon Sinek
Tony Robbins
Sharon Pearson
Tony Hseih
John Maxwell
Richard Branson
Seth Godin
Kate Vitasek
Dave Thompson
Ben Reeves
Jakub Wolanski
Michele Jones
Tamara Burrell
Paul Boone

Key Learnings

Key Learnings

Key Learnings

Key Learnings

Key Learnings

Key Learnings

Key Learnings

Key Learnings

Key Learnings

Key Learnings

Key Learnings

Notes

Notes

Notes

Notes

Notes

Notes

Notes

Notes

Notes

Notes

Notes

Notes

Notes

Notes

Notes

Notes

Notes

Notes

Made in the USA
Lexington, KY
16 February 2016